Timothy Joseph O'Mahony

Joseph Carriere

Timothy Joseph O'Mahony

Joseph Carriere

ISBN/EAN: 9783744664196

Printed in Europe, USA, Canada, Australia, Japan

Cover: Foto ©ninafisch / pixelio.de

More available books at **www.hansebooks.com**

J. O'Mahony

JOSEPH CARRIERE.

[*The Author reserves to himself the right of Translation.*]

JOSEPHUS CARRIÈRE RUTHENSIS,

Vir Simplex ac Rectus,
Veri et æqui Religiosissimus Cultor,
In theologia sacra Doctor, et Scriptor insignis.
Modestia Insignior
Rebus in omnibus prudens; in inspiciendis solers
In exæquendis Constans: secreti Tenax
Quo Superiore
Societas
In regimine Parœciæ S. Sulpitii redintegrata est
Et a Sancta Sede per decretum approbationis solemne
Confirmata
Regularis disciplinæ Zelator Indefessus
In ipso bisitationum cursu obiit Lugdunii,
DIE APRILIS 23, ANNO DOMINI, 1864,
ÆTATIS 69.

[*Inscription engraved upon L'Abbe Carriere's tomb, and also to be seen on the published engravings of his likeness.*]

JOSEPH CARRIERE,

LATE

SUPERIOR-GENERAL OF THE SULPICEANS AND VICAR-GENERAL OF PARIS;

ST. SULPICE

AND

THE CHURCH OF FRANCE

IN HIS TIME.

BY

T. J. O'MAHONY, D. D., D. C. L.,

(*Olim Sti. Sulpitii Alumnus*).

VOS ESTIS SAL TERRÆ.... VOS ESTIS LUX MUNDI.

DUBLIN:
J. MULLANY, 1 PARLIAMENT-STREET.
1865.

TO

HIS BRETHREN IN THE MINISTRY,

This Notice

ON A COMMON FRIEND AND TEACHER,

IS RESPECTFULLY ADDRESSED,

BY

. THE AUTHOR.

PREFACE.

THE following memoir of the late distinguished Superior of Sulpice, being (as explained in the Introduction) not so much a biography as a biographical study, made for the general purpose of exposing and explaining the present condition of the clerical body of France, it can be understood why narrative so often gives place to reflections, and also why, even in the choice of matter for narration, points of general significance as illustrative of L'Abbe Carriere's time, his position, and the body to which he belonged, are dwelt on in preference to details of a more exclusively personal character.

The author is aware that the latter, precisely for being more personal to L'Abbe Carriere, would prove the more interesting for many of his readers, and, for the same reason, would appear the more relevant to the special subject of his work; he feels bound, however, to give preference to the former, as being of more consequence for the general object which he has in view, while, at the same time, in carefully delineating M. Carriere's peculiarities of character, mind, and tastes, he has endeavoured to discharge to the utmost of his power the principal duty which a biographer owes to his subject.

Ardmore Cottage, Carrigaline, Co. Cork.
Feast of St. Isidore, B.D.,
4th April, 1865.

CONTENTS.

	Page.
INTRODUCTION	1

CHAPTER I.
Carriere's early life.—The Spirit of St. Sulpice .. 25

CHAPTER II.
His College Course.—Incidents connected with it.—Muzzarelli.—Cardinal Maury 35

CHAPTER III.
M. Carriere's successful career as Professor and Author.—Censure pronounced by the Holy See on some propositions contained in his writings.—Corrected edition in consequence 47

CHAPTER IV.
M. Carriere's Mission to America.—Assists at the Council of Baltimore.—Elected Superior-General of his Society.. 64

CHAPTER V.
M. Carriere's daily life, habits, and occupations, as Superior of St. Sulpice and General of his Society 73

CHAPTER VI.
France and Rome.—Questions about M. Carriere's sentiments in connexion with both 100

CHAPTER VII.

St. Sulpice 124

CHAPTER VIII.

The " Ecclesiastical Spirit" of French Ecclesiastical Training 144

CHAPTER IX.

Concluding Particulars of M. Carriere's Life,—His Death.. 160

CHAPTER X.

Person, and Character of M. Carriere 173

JOSEPH CARRIERE,

SUPERIOR OF ST. SULPICE.

INTRODUCTION.

WHAT name is now more familiar to students of moral theology, in college or on the mission, than this—the long venerated name of the author of "*De Justitia*," "*De Contractibus*," and "*De Matrimonio?*" Known and quoted wherever Catholic theology has a school, he is the favourite author in most of our colleges for questions, connected with the great practical departments of sacred science on which he wrote; he is constantly referred to in class-hall, or conference-room; while his treatises are the received class-books in some of our colleges here and in America, as they are in nearly all the ecclesiastical seminaries of France. Naturally, therefore, to us all—professors, students, and priests on the mission—"familiar as a household word" has become the name of Carriere of St. Sulpice.

As a peculiarity of these countries, it has been observed that when a celebrated personage—especially one familiar to science or literature—has terminated his career, the public becomes most anxious to know all about him, and every detail connected with his history, or likely to illustrate his character, is eagerly sought after. Thereupon, of course, the magazines of public information—the papers, journals, and reviews of the day—teem with biographical notices, and vie with one another in adding fresh details to the story of the great departed's life, or fresh touches to the recognized picture of his character. So that the public soon becomes as familiar with his personal history and peculiarities, as it had been before with his writings and his name.

Now, Joseph Carriere, so long and so well-known to us all, has been nearly a twelve-months dead; yet what have we heard or read about him? Would it be too much to say that most of us, even of those generally well posted on the news of the day, have never learned even the fact of his death—and this for the obvious reason that our ordinary channels of information contained nothing whatever about him. Nor is this at all surprising in the case of un-Catholic, or even Catholic but purely secular organs. For although Carriere was undeniably for many years an author of world-wide reputation, it must be remembered he was so only in the Church, and not at all in the world. Moreover, he was in every respect emphatically "not of the world;" so (it is the old story) " the world knew him not;" and when he went from it, it had nothing to say about him. Not a lecturer, not a preacher, not even a religious *literateur*, but a theologian, writing in Latin for the benefit of clergymen and clerical students only, he was a purely ecclesiastical celebrity, whose fame was confined to strictly clerical circles, and whose life, in consequence, could not be expected to possess such interest for the general English reader, even though Catholic, as might claim for it a place in his newspaper. Besides, however, our purely secular or general newspapers, have we not journals and other publications of a sufficiently religious character to justify our regarding them as at least semi-clerical, and as such, having undertaken the responsibility of giving subjects of considerable ecclesiastical interest? To these, surely, we were entitled to look for what should necessarily be of such interest to all members of the clerical body as a biographical notice of one of our greatest and best known of modern theologians after death had closed his distinguished career. Of these religious Catholic organs, then, at least, we have reason to complain that no such notice of Carriere has at any time since his death appeared—at least, we have never seen any, though we anxiously looked out for it; still further, that we were left in ignorance of even the fact of his decease. Let it not be objected that he was, after all, a foreigner. A doctor of such authority in the Church, an ecclesiastical author of such wide-spread renown, should be regarded as a foreigner in no land where studies a Catholic student or lives a Catholic priest; besides, to do them justice, our religious Catholic journals seldom leave us in ignorance of ordinary foreign events of ecclesiastical interest, which makes their omission, in this instance, the more remarkable.

The fact of M. Carriere having been left thus long unnoticed, and now so likely to be hopelessly passed over amongst us, must be the present writer's apology for taking on himself to pay this tribute to his memory—a tribute which he believes to be a sacred debt, nowhere more due to him, outside his native land, than in English-speaking countries, where he is universally esteemed as an author, and to a great extent even personally known and revered.* Moreover, the author must confess it is

* Very many clergymen now on the mission in England, Scotland, and the colonies, and not a few even in Ireland, have had

a debt which, in default of any one else taking it up, personal gratitude laid at his own door to discharge.

While doing so, however, he may be permitted to give expression to broader and higher views than the sole prospect of satisfying the curiosity of persons anxious to know all that can be told them of an old and esteemed acquaintance. He ventures, therefore, to express a hope, that in the present little work (as he endeavoured to do in a previous publication illustrative of the character of a late distinguished churchman), he has done a something, little though it be, towards making the ecclesiastical body, to which he is proud of belonging, somewhat better known as to its existing state, and consequently better appreciated, at least by his brethren in the ministry, to whose kind indulgence he commits this notice on a common friend, and to whom he principally addresses himself throughout. Who will undertake works of this description if not one of ourselves ? and, at the same time, who can be expected to do them justice so well as one of us, who best know the ways of the sanctuary ? Yet

Carriere as professor or superior; the same may be said of still greater numbers in North America and Canada; indeed, in both these countries, several of the most distinguished and influential ecclesiastics of the day have been students of St. Sulpice, of course in his time.

such works are eminently useful in those days and in those English-speaking countries, if to no other purpose to keep alive that self-respect which we owe to ourselves, as members of the great Catholic priesthood. The English press is so ready to seize on every little defect, and make market of the merest slip of the least member of our body; so many English writers there are busy in publishing its apparent faults and failures, while so very few are found to draw attention to its countless admirable members, its manifold intrinsic perfections, or its daily triumphs and its glories. Let a trifling disorder begin to show itself somewhere throughout its vast extent, or a weakness come over some unimportant member, and soon we are made familiar with every circumstance connected with the tale of folly or shame. None are naturally more impressed with such details than we whom they most interest; and the consequence is that, thanks to the very secular, in most respects un-Catholic, in many even un-Christian, nature of our English channels of information, we are seldom left in ignorance of what in anywise could tend to lessen our self-esteem. Accustomed to see ourselves so much through the darkened glasses lent by the world for our personal inspection—its Jewish telegrams and the coloured communications of its anti-Catholic organs, like so many magnifying lenses continually held up to our eyes, and directed against every little excrescence of the human element that may happen to rise upon our body—the consequence must be that our view of it should tend to grow vitiated. So frequently forced to dwell on the little it must occasionally present of what is unamiable and feeble, we may, unless on our guard, insensibly glide into a something like practical forgetfulness of the infallible health of its everlasting youth, or, conscious of its past excellencies, fall into a sort of drowsy insensibility to the present charms of its all-surpassing beauty, to the present matchless proportions of its superhuman strength, to its evidences of present indomitable energy, and to the certainty which, even to human eye, its features still present of everlasting vigour. Circumstanced as we are, it is hardly to be expected that we should not have at least a tendency towards this lamentable oblivion, and that some of us—especially the more mixed up in the world and best read in modern English literature— should not be more or less tainted with those theories of "growing decrepitude," "well-meaning but antiquated ways," "intemperate zeal," "unseasonable intolerance," &c., which are now so much in vogue concerning the Church, among the better disposed liberal Protestants and a certain class of would-be liberal Catholic writers. We have, therefore, no reason to be surprised that your " highly respectable" clergyman of the brilliant and liberal type—more polished than solid, more *liberal,* as the saying is, than *ultramontane,* habituated to views of the Church, not as she is to-day, but as the world now shows her—should occasionally be led (while at heart a sound Catholic and worthy priest) to give expression to general sentiments of distrust and vexation, or even to ill-concealed feeling of shame, touching the body to which he belongs. Yet what more deserves to be combatted—for what is more pitiable—than the presence of such feelings in any of its members towards such a body ? The clerical body of the Catholic Church ! that which, as a body, even its enemies must admit, as they have over and over confessed, to be the most perseveringly consistent, the most uniformly noble, the most preternaturally pure, and now, after centuries of combatted existence, the most invulnerable still—the greatest and the mightiest the world ever saw. Nor let us for over-delicacy hesitate in declaring it (happy necessity as it is of our profession—most special obligation consequent on our momentary duties as *dispensatores sacrorum*)—a body which we know to be, amongst the habitual sin-defiled "children of men," as "the lily among thorns;" notwithstanding its many venial faults and certain unamiable imperfections peculiar to itself, always showing fresh and fair to the eye of heaven in its all-redeeming brightness of habitual state of grace—that working dress of its daily life, which few of its members (while remaining such) do ever dare lay aside, or, if ever, under sacrilege's awful penalty must immediately resume. To regard such a body with feelings other than of grateful admiration, is surely nothing short of a crying injustice to ourselves; and as it can only be the result of a vitiated view, such as the world of English literature makes to itself, and is actively engaged in spreading around, whatever tends to counteract it should be looked on as a boon suited to the peculiar circumstances of our country and our time.

There are spots in the sun, and, judging from the size they present at our distance from that planet, they must be pretty large spots too—some thousands of miles of dark extent. We, however, who can see the whole, lose sight of its few petty blemishes in the dazzling brilliancy of its general mass, and unanimously agree in pronouncing the sun a body of light—our ideal type of all that is bright, and grandly beautiful. Would that the world did treat so fairly the mystic body of the Sun of Justice. Its policy, however, is to direct attention only to its few dark spots, and while fixing thereon the gaze to publish aloud : " Lo ! it is darkness all !"

" It is necessary that scandals be" in the Church, nor can its sanctuary be exempt from them ; under the eyes of its Founder a crying one defiled it, small as it then was, and all of His own selection. Why should not such things be there now ? Such things are there, and must be to the end of time. Yet, as Luther loved to repeat (to his own and to his party's condemnation, the Catholics took care to retort), the Priesthood of the New Law must be (as a body) a holy nation and a pure race—a people after Jehovah's own heart. The enemies of the Catholic Church can therefore use no better tactics than to show forth *her* priesthood as far otherwise; not that they pretend to claim for any body of their own such priestly traits, but because for heresy it suffices to *protest*—for infidelity to *deny*. Their point is merely to prove that the Catholic clergy is not the promised priesthood of the New Law ; they cannot, for they dare not, claim that honour for any other. With true worldly-wise prudence, therefore, scandals taken, or purported to be taken, from the sanctuary have always been the favourite arms of the adversaries of Catholicity. Naturally, too, they have always proved the most successful in doing it harm, for they strike at its very heart's core; and their use turns to account that most available weakness of the human mind, a tendency to jump from the particular to the general. The heretical sophisms of the reformers would have gone a poor way in their work of deformation but for their scandal pictures and scandal stories. Well they knew it; and their popular preachers never thought of presenting an argument against popery without having previously garnished it, *à la* Luther, with abundant scandal matter of the most savoury description. To come down to our own times, every one accustomed to surmount the difficulties which Protestants encounter in their conversion, is aware that those eternal topics of English literature—mediæval convent licentiousness, monkish *gourmandize* and intemperance, and general priestly wickedness, go farther to alienate such persons' minds from our Church, than the sacrifices demanded by her obligations of human nature, or by her dogmas of human reason. Ah! indeed, the human mind would have lost its peculiarities and the world its prejudices, if the scandal-teeming telegrams of the day, and the letters of anti-Catholic *specials* from the Continent, did not drive a thriving trade in their business of misrepresentation, even with worthy souls—for notwithstanding their acquired worth, these good souls retain their essential nature, and still are human.

While, therefore, her enemies are busy picking up every particle of scandal they can find, to exhibit as samples of the material now-a-days to be found in the Church, that son of hers, we imagine, does a needful work who helps to bring forth some of those treasures of edification with which her bosom is at all times teeming, and a grain of whose golden masses will do more to give the lie to misrepresentations as to her present constitution than volumes of laboured *a priori* apologies, or of direct refutations.

It has been said (at least in substance) by a well-disposed philosopher of the free-Catholic school, that the Church must now rely for attractions on the unimpaired features of her divine element—as we may say, of her heaven-sent *soul*—the strength and beauty of her dogmas, and the purity of her moral teaching; but that as to her body, "the flesh hath corrupted its way," and inspection of its members is now likely to be productive only of disappointment or disgust.

Due allowance made for its human element, Christ's mystic body, if but fairly regarded, can never inspire feelings such as those, no matter under what aspect it be taken. The body of the faithful has, no doubt, deteriorated; yet such as it still is, what other in the world (all things considered) can be said to equal it in all that constitutes Christian perfection? In point of fact, outside its pale there is no body that deserves the name of "faithful" at all. We freely confess, however, that since the "ages of faith," the lay element of the Church has sadly suffered in beauty and healthful vigour. But when was her ecclesiastical element (that which most intimately constitutes the organs of her life) fairer to look on, healthier, or more active? When did her religious houses present less scandal? When was there, in her religious orders, in her congregations, or in her societies, less licentiousness, less simony, less spirit of disobedience? When was her clergy less mercenary, less extravagant, less luxurious, more chaste, or more zealous for God's glory and the good of souls, than at the present day? Or would it be too much to say, in view of the time-made changes of her two-fold element—her clergy and her laity—that what the Church has lost in one way, she has gained, to a certain extent, in another—if not in positive increase of exalted perfection, in more general immunity from impurities. So that, among the changes which the lapse of nigh two thousand years standing have wrought within her ancient edifice, should be reckoned a certain interchange of the relative aspects of its sanctuary and the body of its vast enclosure, with regard to the more sensible and impressive evidence of that sanctity which must always be found shining inside.* Nave and aisles present not an appearance so well filled nor so respectable as before; and even of the congregation that is there, too many, alas! more than of old, are now seen to turn their backs upon the altar, and their eyes from its sights, and their ears from its sounds. Then, looking among the crowd, much will meet the eye that is painful and offensive, which used not be seen there, and whose misplaced presence is due—not to any imperfection of the building, nor to the negligence of those who have care of its well-keeping, but to the *men* who defile the one and disregard the other. Yes (though we believe there is a great improvement in it since the last

* Such, we know, would be old Peter Damian's conviction if he lived again in these days, and such will, we believe, be the conclusion of a careful comparison between the "manifestoes" of a Gregory VII. and the "encyclicals" of a Pius IX., in the views each presents of the clergy and faithful of his own time.

century), we allow that the body of the faithful is not at all so edifying to-day as it was in the good old Catholic times. But, on the other hand, look at the sanctuary! Is that not as fair to see, as efficiently furnished and well administered, at least, as ever? While, moreover, does it not look even more cleanly now, and as a whole more edifying, than when the vast body of the sacred enclosure was more cheering to behold? Aye, and still further to dare a comparison with the "ages of faith" in that very point which, as, it most distinguishes, most endears them to us—when was the *faith* of the clergy, and of all the religious bodies, male and female, more simple, more hearty, or purer, than it is to-day? One may impugn the zeal, integrity, or even the moral correctness of a priest or religious : who, now-a-days, ever thinks of casting doubts on their faith? "Respectful doubt," remarks a modern reviewer, "is the most that, in this enlightened age, can be asked of the generality of men; there is seldom sincerity in any other profession of faith." Speaking of what he knew, the man spoke a sad truth. Outside the Church, we are convinced it is so with the greatest part of the world. "This is an age of all but universal and still fast-gaining scepticism," exclaims a distinguished Protestant dignitary; and we have no doubt it is so for the clergy to which he belongs—the half Puseyite, half Voltairean, or "undecided" ministers of Protestant communions. But for the clergy—but for the religious bodies of the Catholic Church, this reason-mad nineteenth century is AN AGE OF FAITH as thoroughly as was the age of crusaders, pilgrims, and altar-loving princes. The vaunted faith of a Godfrey de Bouillon, for the first time approaching the "holy places," was not a whit more simple, more lively, or truer in principle or in feeling than that of your lately ordained priest going up the altar steps, with fearful soul and glowing heart, to celebrate his first mass; nor was it even more impressive in its display than that which we know fills the soul, as we have seen it to overflow the tearful eyes of our present saintly Pontiff, Pius, when, for public profession of faith in that mysterious presence which, more than any other object of Catholic belief, taxes reason and demands sacrifices of sense, he is borne in solemn procession around the piazza of St. Peter's—his head resting on the remonstrance wherein faith says "Jesus is laid"—his figure motionless in rapt adoration—and with that about him, in feature and in bearing, which, be each one's individual creed what it may, forces upon every beholder of the nations assembled there a conviction, common to all, that the man they look upon FEELS HE IS WITH HIS GOD. Yes, we must maintain that, examined by the double criterion of Christian perfection, lively living faith, on the one hand, and existing morality on the other, the Church has no reason to decline serious inspection as to the actual state of her members, and it is most false that in her "the flesh hath so corrupted its way" that in prudence she should avoid the searching eye of philosophical or statistical observers. On the contrary, as to her clerical body in particular—as we may call it, her inmost self—she has many reasons to invite the mutual observation of her children and the scrutiny of outsiders.

Is there not, for instance, in the very fact of seeing the Church *as she is*, much that is reassuring to those within her bosom and attractive to those as yet without?

Somehow or other, one cannot help feeling that people were almost naturally good in the "good old Catholic times," when, even in the world, piety seemed quite *à la mode*. As for the early ages of the Church, the very atmosphere seems to us now to have been so impregnated with sanctity, that a saint, one is almost inclined to think, must have been the normal state of a Christian—at least of one who, in those bleak times, would never outgrow the proportions of a sound Catholic or a pious person. Hence we find that earnest souls of a certain practical temperament will gladly turn from viewing the heroic martyrs and taumathurgical saints of old to the more congenial, because perhaps more intelligible, and certainly more imitable models of modern sanctity. So, it cannot be doubted that many good Christians will still more anxiously look out for the "men of the day," and inquire into what they are even with more interest than they would inspect specimens of canonized virtue, modern, it is true, but yet belonging to other days than those in which they live. And is not the feeling natural? Certainly children all of the same Catholic Church, catholic in time as in space—sons of the one noble house and members of the same family—great and good brethren, ancient, modern, or contemporary, should all inspire us with a family interest. Whilst, however, bestowing all due regard on the old family pictures that deck the walls of our common home— while even regarding with very special interest the traits of those who lately lived there, but not in our time, is it not natural that we inquire with a most peculiar interest into the actual state of our family, such as it is to-day? Moreover, is it not to be expected that in these treacherous times, when calumnies and exaggerations are so much abroad respecting its members, certain advantages of a cheering, doubt-dispelling, and consequently desirable kind, are to be derived from this habitual self-inspection, seeing that its results must be, as we maintain, so satisfactory?

Then, with regard to those inquirers who from without (some, to be sure, with evil, jealous eyes, but also some with simply curious gaze, or even with wistful glances) are always peering in at one side or the other, "to see what is inside the Church, and of what kind it is, especially up about the altar"—with regard to *outsiders*, we doubt very much that it would be productive of more practical good to draw attention to our time-honoured pictures of (say, for instance) the wondrous physico-moral achievements of the saints of the desert, or to our glorious models of mediæval sanctity, all radiant with a supernatural glory, or even to our striking likenesses of modern saints—undeniably authentic as these all may be proved—than to point to such every-day living realities as may be seen moving, full of life and activity, within the Church to-day, in and about her sanctuary—to the angelic forms of our choirs of "consecrated virgins" of every order—in particular, the busy, self-sacrificing Sisters of Charity and Mercy; the active but ascetic members of our religious bodies of men—the devoted Christian Brothers, for instance, and their like; or, to come to the clergy and to some of their specialities, to the enthusiastic missionary, lonely wanderer, or fixed workman—the personally modest and humble, but apostolically daring and indefatigable French *curé*—the highly ecclesiastical and noble-spirited, but simple-hearted Spanish father—the priestly, correct, earnest, and learned German clergyman—the church-loving, ascetic Italian *padre;* not forgetting (though we say it, who should not) the proverbially short-lived, because really hard-worked and hardship-worn, but ever cheerful poor Irish curate, &c. &c.; and, since "Rome" is the reputed "eye-sore," "insurmountable plague-spot," and so on, of Catholicity—to the really edifying, poorly-paid, but hard-working and remarkably abstemious members of the local Church and court of Rome—at least, such as it undeniably is to-day, with its ever-busy, simple-living cardinals, and its present irreproachable Head. If the inquirer be rather of a universal and philosophical turn of mind, let him, we should say, look to the general facts of the purity of life, simplicity of habits, with its cause or consequence, a striking absence of great individual wealth, comparatively high standard of education, and consequent universal enlightenment, lively faith, apostolic zeal, life, and energy, generally observable at the present time throughout the world-wide extent of the sanctuary of the Catholic Church, among its countless, multiform ecclesiastical bodies, secular and religious. Or if he be of the new practical, comparison-seeking school, by all means, let him follow his bent. Let him compare the Catholic clergy as it is with any other class of men on earth to-day, and let the comparison be with regard to all that may be supposed to constitute a good man, or, still better, with regard to the acknowledged characteristics of a good Christian—purity and simplicity of life, habits of self-denial, and the spirit of prayer. The comparison would perhaps be hardly fair with any body of laymen—then let it be with the clergymen of any other communion, not alone in the distinguishing traits of a disciple, but in the natural marks of a *minister* of Christ, particularly in what we are agreed to call the apostolic spirit—its self-sacrifice and religious zeal. The result of such comparisons is not doubtful, and a Catholic has every reason to encourage them.

Indeed, taking into account the practical notions and " comparative" tendencies of the age in which we live, it is very probable that no more powerful apologies for the Church's divine superiority over all would-be Christian sects could be offered to a serious "inquirer," from within or without her bosom, than a correct idea of the essential nature of her priesthood, illustrated by a well-directed view of its actual condition, the details of its daily life, and its general character as it now lies spread over the universe. Not only, therefore, as presenting antidotes of the surest kind to the poisonous effect of modern English literature, and as correctives of its vitiated daily news on all that regards the Catholic clergy, but even as calculated to afford practical edification to minds of every class, works appertaining to contemporary ecclesiastical history are most desirable in these English-speaking countries, and in these treacherous times. Such works, as exposing the present life of her sanctuary, serve to bring into light the real state of the Church; and, as we set out by saying, to make the Catholic Church with its clergy better known, is to make it better appreciated, more loved, and more esteemed.

The hope of doing something towards an end naturally so dear to the heart of a priest, led us in a former publication to draw attention, on the occasion of his death, to the late lamented Cardinal Morlot, chief prelate of the most influential Church in the world, next to Rome, and, at the same time, a fair sample (at least by his character and *spirit*) of that vast clerical body which exercises such immense influence in the ecclesiastical world by its spiritual literature, its institutions, its organized societies, and its armies of foreign missionaries. The same consideration now gives us reason to trust, that we are engaged in something more congenial to our personal tastes and to the spirit of our profession than a mere work of literature, while drawing up the present notice of one who must be regarded as the greatest modern theologian of this same great Church of France—for many years the head of her principal establishment for the education of her clergy, the superior-general of a community to whose care is entrusted a vast number of her clerical colleges throughout the empire, and who was himself the teacher or spiritual father of a large proportion of her existing hierarchy, as he continued through life in many ways their highly-respected adviser.

Appearing now *eleven* months after his death, we feel that this notice on Carriere does come rather late; but also we hasten to declare what we confessed before—that is precisely why it comes from *us*. After waiting in vain up to the present time to see such a notice appear in some form or other, we feared that it would never come at all; and as we considered its subject not yet devoid of interest (at least for our brethren in the ministry, whom only at any time it could be expected to interest), we decided on taking the task into our own hands, though it *was* in the eleventh hour—for, thought we, " better late than never."

The life of an eminent French ecclesiastic, of which more than fifty years were spent in Paris and most of that time in the direction of such a community as the Sulpiceans, at the head of such an establishment as St. Sulpice), should necessarily present features of more general interest than those only relative to his *personal* history. In justice to himself, the author must say that he has kept this in view, and has acted upon it within the limits in which his plan confined him. That plan being a very limited one (for the present, at least), his work could not have been otherwise—in fact, he presents it rather as a biographical *picture* of a priest than as a narrative of the life of a distinguished man. At the same time, he must plead guilty to having done his best as far as he went; and while painfully sensible of his little work presenting many deficiencies and still more imperfections, to have endeavoured to make it as complete and interesting as, under the circumstances of its composition, he possibly could.

CHAPTER I.

CARRIERE'S EARLY LIFE.—THE SPIRIT OF ST. SUL-PICE, &c.

JOSEPH CARRIERE was born on the 19th of February, 1795, in a little village of the diocese of Rodez. At a very early age, he entered the college of St. Affrique, where he remained until his preparatory or school studies were completed. After leaving St. Affrique, we find him engaged in the capacity of professor, or rather usher, in a small college *d'instruction secondaire* at Amiens. In this position, so honorable for one of his extreme youth, it appears that he gave the greatest satisfaction; in fact, displayed a tact and discernment far beyond his years. (He must have been yet very young, for he afterwards completed his course of theology before having at all attained the age required for priesthood.) Here, too, the young teacher gave early proofs of those powers of communicating information, and clearly fixing in the mind, which in after life so distinguished him as professor and author. After a stay of three years at Amiens, where, whilst discharging his duties as teacher, he continued to perfect himself in the knowledge of *belles-lettres* and philosophy, he entered, as regular student and aspirant to the priesthood, the archdiocesan college of St. Sulpice, Paris, and began the usual course of theology on the 19th of August, 1812. Well it was for him, and for the Church of France in which he was called to have such extensive influence, that the critical task of training his heart and mind fell to the lot of such an orthodox house as this, where the anti-Roman, not to say un-Catholic principles then purposely set afloat, never found a footing, and where the dangerous imperial or parliamentary principles of even a certain portion of the clergy were studiously combatted—well, we say, it was for young Carriere that, in those days of occasional clerical weakness, he fell into the hands of the Sulpiceans, of whom not a member (spread, though they were, over France) could be got to sign the insidious *Constitution Civile d'Clergé*, which so many of the clergy had been at the time prevailed on to take up. And here let us enter a little into the spirit or general state of feeling which prevailed in this house when our young student entered it, and which, of course, in general with his fellow-students, he failed not to imbibe.

It was hardly a year after the death of M. Emery, who had been such a long time superior of St. Sulpice, and who is so famous in the ecclesiastical annals of the age as the uncompromising defender of

Catholic principles at the imperial court, during the re-organization of the Church in France after the Revolution. The memory of their old superior, yet green in the college, naturally made his spirit fresh and strong amongst the students and professors. What could it have been, this spirit of Bonaparte's unflinching antagonist in that monarch's encroachments on Church authority, of the old priest who resisted, notwithstanding the submission of local church dignitaries, but, as it proved to be, a spirit of Catholic independence ?—in details of practice, a confident self-reliance founded on fixedness of doctrine—in general conduct and in principle, a chivalrous devotion to the one unerring authority of Peter's See.* Nor was this spirit of Emery, then prevalent in the house, other than a *feature* of the old, unchanging spirit of St. Sulpice suited to the exigencies of the occasion.

The community of St. Sulpice having taken for its model, as best suited to the special nature of a priest's preparation for the mission, the hidden life

* Cardinal Wiseman, in his "Recollections of the Last Four Popes," remarks, referring to Napoleon: " He was ill advised by those who should have been his counsellors, who, with a *single exception*, left uncorrected, or rather seconded the feeling which experience had made a second nature—that being irresistible, he should not be resisted." That single exception, the Cardinal adds in a note, was " L'Abbé Emery—and Napoleon respected and honoured him for it."—*Page* 49.

of Jesus at Nazareth,* was from its foundation, and still is, characterized by a spirit of submissiveness to authority complete and uncomplaining—shunning anything like opposition, even when justifiable, and moreover studiously avoiding whatever might tend to bring upon it public attention. Opportunities (especially during and since the French Revolution) have not been wanting to put to the test the real nature of this "spirit of the house," as it was commonly called. When such occasions presented themselves, the community of St. Sulpice failed not in proving that its "reserve" was not cowardice, nor its "obedience" weakness of principle, but that both—sterling ecclesiastical virtues—were taken from Him, whose life of privacy and subjection its members had made the model of their own, in its lengthened preparation for the public preaching of the Gospel. An occasion of the kind we refer to existed during the presidency of M. Emery, and at the time of M. Carriere's entrance into the house. Of a less formidable nature than that of the Revolution, it was a time of real danger for the Church of France, a time when, while its local authorities were being reinstated, principles obnoxious to the universal authority of its supreme Pontiff were being busily revived; and worse than all, when mem-

* A special feast, commemorative of the hidden life of Christ, is one of the principal festivals of the community.

bers of its clergy, whose exalted positions made them the ordinary guides of their inferior brethren, were daily more and more giving way to that bane of regular discipline, that blight of sound clerical conduct, *the force of exigencies*, and thereupon making repeated sacrifice of principle under plausible pretexts of necessity. Adhesion to known principles, persevering even to determined resistance if necessary (regulated, of course, by constant attention to the ordinances of the Supreme Pastor), much more than a spirit of obedience to ordinary superiors, was now to be looked for in sound ecclesiastical bodies, and *was* found in that of St. Sulpice. Nor could its traditional spirit be said to have changed for the time. It was still that of the Thirty-years Life, only presenting that particular feature of it which in his boyhood brought Jesus out before the authorities of the synagogue—before those whom he was the first to acknowledge as the appointed doctors of the law, but with whom he thought fit to "dispute" in obedience to a higher authority than theirs—the will of his Father.

That this spirit of resistance to power when principle was involved, to the authority of even local church dignitaries though supported by the state, when the authority of the Church's Head was being lessened, really is a feature of the professed "spirit of St. Sulpice," manifesting itself whenever due emergencies have arisen, no one acquainted with the French ecclesiastical annals of the last two centuries need be informed. Who would wish to investigate the matter need only glance at the history of the house immediately previous to the time of our sketch, or may even take it at the precise period which occupies us.

It will be remembered, for instance, how, in the famous disputes relative to the "Civil Constitution of the Clergy," at the breaking out of the great Revolution, in the serious affair of the "organic articles" at the beginning of the Empire, in the still more important matter of the "canonical institutions of the bishops" in 1809, and in the great question of "capitular jurisdiction," &c. &c., that is to say, in all the questions of the day, the side of the Holy See was emphatically that of St. Sulpice, though forced on this account to take stand against authorities clerical as well as secular; while, in the person of its superior, M. Emery, the interests of Rome found their chief, their almost only defender at the French court, at the time when the natural protectors of the Church's rights in France were giving way before the strong will of Napoleon. Nor must we forget (inasmuch as it belongs to the very time of our sketch) the attitude of reserve maintained by the Sulpiceans of Paris towards their reputed ordinary, Cardinal Maury, even before that prelate's condemnation, a conduct, we need hardly say, fraught with danger to their community. In the person of the subject of our notice himself, whilst yet a student, we shall have to bring forward a very striking example of the force of this truly Catholic state of feeling in the house.

But it may be said, all this refers to a remarkably peculiar period—in fact, to the one brilliant page in the history of St. Sulpice. We answer that when similar emergencies arose, similar dispositions failed not to be shown, as well before that time as since. We go so far back as the time of Fenelon, when the intellectual disease of Jansenism was making such ravages amongst the fairest and stoutest minds of France. The gentle bishop of Cambrai is fired with a holy wrath at the sight of the increasing number of its victims; in pastoral after pastoral he denounces the defaulters; and in one, the most finished of them all, after a long list of the orders, societies, and congregations then being more or less tainted by the malevolent disorder, he concludes in those remarkable words, which, coming from Fenelon, speak volumes for our point: "In fact, the community of St. Sulpice alone seems to have had the heart to keep thoroughly clear of the contagion, *and therefore his eminence the Cardinal Archbishop thinks but little of them, and does not like them at all.*"* Finally, under the govern-

* *See* Rohrbacher, Hist. de l'Egise; art. Fenelon.

ment of the restoration, almost in our own times, when M. Carriere professed there, the seminary became actually a "suspected house" with the state authorities, because its teaching was notoriously opposed to the old Gallican theories on the limits of Church authority, which the government was at the time busily engaged in diffusing.

These facts, and many more that we could instance, are so many unanswerable proofs for those who need them, that the famous " spirit of St. Sulpice," though one of reserve, has nothing in common with pusillanimity; though one of perfect obedience, is by no means one of unapostolic weakness, listlessness, or fear; that, moreover, on all due occasions it has distinguished itself by a striking readiness to side with the Holy See, even in questions where room was left for doubt, and (what those who are unacquainted with the traditions of the company may be inclined to doubt) on occasions where national honor was to be sacrificed, and even local ecclesiastical superiors were to be opposed.

The above remarks may seem unnecessarily digressive, but they are not so. In justice to him whose life and character we have undertaken to expose, we are bound to make it understood that his *Alma Mater*, the chief nurse of his young mind and heart, was, in those critical times for him and for the Church, what she should have been. Then,

Carriere is in every way so identified with St. Sulpice, that to expose the principles and ways of that house is to give an idea of those he followed. At the same time, since the opportunity of referring to it presented itself, it was well to have shown that the educational body to which is entrusted the formation of a vast proportion of the French clergy, and which, moreover, outside its own seminaries, by its standard college works of piety (almost the only ones used by seminarians), and by its class-books, found more or less in every college for priests throughout the country, has gained universal influence on the formation of the ecclesiastical mind in France—really is a nurse of perfectly sound constitution, which no disease, however prevalent, has at any time affected, and which still continues vigorous and healthful as ever. Therefore it is that, in answer to the sinister doubts now so much insinuated by the un-Catholic English press, as to the perfect orthodoxy of certain influential portions of the "Gallican" priesthood, and to the silly hints thrown out, in consequence, of powerful attempts being made to shake, and if possible to remove, the allegiance of her ELDEST DAUGHTER from Mother Rome, we are proud to reply, there is, there can be no cause for alarm from within or without, because the spirit which moves in the Church of France to-day, and is now being infused into the young members of her nascent clergy for her future life and action, is no other than the SPIRIT OF ST. SULPICE; and that spirit, history's sure testimony guarantees to have been—as they who, like ourselves, have felt it, must pronounce still to be—possessed of all the essentials for a perfect priest—with the saints' love for silence, retirement, peace, and obedience to all constituted power; the apostles' zeal, when duty calls, to dare and to do; the confessors' readiness, when needful, to proclaim the truth, and to stand by it; the martyrs' courage in the hour of danger, not the less real because unprovokingly calm; and, above all, the Catholic's unflinching devotion to the interests of the Holy See, not the less deep because in its *ordinary* course flowing noiseless and smooth.

CHAPTER II.

HIS COLLEGE COURSE.—INCIDENTS CONNECTED WITH IT.—MUZZARELLI.—CARDINAL MAURY.

WHILE Joseph Carriere was quietly pursuing his studies in St. Sulpice, he formed an acquaintance which, although its object was unconnected with the college, must have had considerable influence on the early turn of his theological convictions, and even in the particular colouring of his views on the politico-religious questions of the day. The circumstance is therefore worthy of notice; its details are moreover interesting, as illustrative of this peculiar period, and even, to some extent, of the natural disposition of our young student. Pope Pius VII. had been lately torn from his throne and people, and all who were supposed to have been his private friends or advisers were doomed either to prison or exile. Amongst the steadiest advisers of the exiled Pontiff in his maintenance of the rights of the Church was known to have been the celebrated theologian, Muzzarelli, who was accordingly banished from Rome, as his totally unpolitical character was an obstacle to his imprisonment. Like many others, seeking a refuge in France, he came to Paris about the time of M. Carriere's entrance into college there, and took humble lodgings in the Rue St. Jacques, bent on prosecuting these theological labours to which had already been devoted the greater part of his life, and to which the political disturbance that drove him from his home proved but a short interruption.

It has been said that the best defence of the state of the French clergy previous to its dispersion by the great Revolution, is to point to the subsequent conduct and lives of its members whilst in exile.

So say we of the court of Rome previous to the political catastrophe which, at the beginning of this century, tore it open to the gaze of the world, exposed its Head to the scrutiny of a wily court, and drove its officers out upon society. We care to offer no other proof of the healthy state of the body of the court, or, it may be said, of the local Church of Rome, than to point to the lives of its members scattered over Europe. As its component parts showed themselves in its dismemberment, so must it have been before in its integrity—a pious and zealous, withal, an active and enlightened body of men. The lives in exile, under every species of discouragement and temptation, of a Pius VII., a Consalvi, a Pacca, a Muzzarelli, &c., are the best of panegyrics on the body they represent. Muzzarelli's life, in particular, whilst in Paris, though one of retirement, was one of unremitting literary toil— a toil which literally ceased only with his death, and even slackened but a very short time before it.

Now the college of St. Sulpice (as it still does) then presented a community in which habits of almost monastic retirement were allied to the studious activity of a university. A place, therefore, of all others suited to Muzzarelli's peculiar tastes, it soon became his habitual, indeed his almost only place of resort. For here as a priest, still more as a theologian, but above all, as the once private friend and now fellow-sufferer in exile of the Holy Father, he found himself amongst admiring friends, in communion with appreciating minds and sympathizing hearts. Young Carriere (who had already attracted considerable attention from his superiors) came in a special manner under the notice of the illustrious visitor. Kindred spirits had met; and notwithstanding disparity of age, still more of position, acquaintance soon ripened into friendship; friendship, as it invariably does, begot interchange of ideas; when (we are told) the veteran doctor, struck with his young friend's nice power of discrimination, coupled, as it not always is, to real depth of judgment, not only took him into his literary confidence, but actually made him a partner in his theological labours.

Great men all long for appreciation. It is a providential instinct with genius, this eager desire to exhibit its offspring or share the fruits of its labour with those who can relish them truly. At the same time, what young mind, thirsting for knowledge, will not thrill with delight at the thought of being able unimpeded to drink of a fountain whose springs it knows to be long-tried, pure wells of the science it loves? It is simply human, this two-fold feeling— or we should rather say, it is natural, and hence universal; but nowhere is it, or can it be, so strong as in the Catholic Church. For here the mellowing influence of age gives a special value to vessels of science, while youth lends a particular charm to its eager aspirants. The delight of an old professor holding forth to a really good class, or satisfying the queries of a deservedly favourite student, is proverbial; and (*we* ask it of all *young* ecclesiastics) what keener enjoyment, what truer, can well be conceived, than, in that free communion of thought which only friendship allows, to sit for hours with some great doctor of the day—a living "*sanctæ ecclesiæ lumen*"—"putting objections," "sounding theories," or, above all, listening to that music of sacred science, which only its great doctors can safely venture on giving out—the endless variety of the "congruities," "possibilities," and "probabilities" almost too beautiful, it sometimes seems, for certainty here, and the certain, but, to the young mind, ever new *necessary* truths of theological conclusions? Ah! yes; we need not to be told of the high intellectual enjoyments, and, at least for the younger one, the delightful fruits born of the frequent communings of those two great minds. As also it is pleasant to reflect that the older of the two must have found therein some consolation for the much he had lost—that in the company of this one truly kindred spirit he must have found at least a partial substitute for that illustrious society, the learned and the saintly, he once enjoyed in the halls, the libraries, and the palaces, or in the college and convent cloisters of his own loved " City of the Soul"—his native Rome.

The happy effect of this intercourse with the great Roman doctor upon the studies of the young French student would have made itself felt at any time, but must have proved especially beneficial in those days of revived and pampered Gallicanism. Indeed, to the well-known teaching and the then existing spirit of his college, we would add this *fact* as guarantee for the sound, orthodox nature of M. Carriere's early training, as affecting the subsequent spirit of his writings. That he was always thoroughly Catholic in doctrine, and orthodox, at least in principle, no one ever dared to deny. But even amongst those who give him credit, as all who know him must, for unimpeachable sincerity of inquiry, there are many who think fit to suspect him as a theologian of Gallican tendencies, due, it has been said, to " first impressions," and the inevitable effect on his yet unmatured mind of the prevailing sentiments of the

French clergy at the time of his college course. Those who think thus of the effects of his "early training" must assuredly (to say no more) be ignorant of the fact of his early intercourse with the adviser of Pius VII. ; or, aware of it, must not advert to its consequence, and do not, therefore, duly realize the fact that M. Carriere's "first impressions" on the various points of sacred science, especially regarding the vexed questions of the day, were highly influenced by him who had so much to do with the direction of his studies and the bias thereby given to his mind—his friend and, we may well say, master, Muzzarelli, the then great light of the Roman school.

At least in the Church, the greatest men are also the best. Great heads and good hearts, or what amounts to the same, masterly minds and virtuous, kindly souls, go together. From his college days down to the declining years of his life, when we knew and admired him, M. Carriere afforded a strikingly happy proof of the truth of this ; and we who knew him as the kind old superior of St. Sulpice, can only say, "it was like him," when we read, that as he was Muzzarelli's frequent companion in his hours of labour, so he proved his constant, watchful attendant during the illness which terminated his career ; and that, amongst the many who had reason to grieve for his death, the illustrious exile found no more sensibly afflicted mourner than the young student of St. Sulpice, who, with tearful eyes, followed after the bier that bore his friend's remains to their foreign grave in Vaugirard.

Although he had not yet completed his course, the time had now come when, according to the custom of the house, young Carriere should be promoted to holy orders, but *he refused to take any just then.* The unreasoned *feeling* of a scrupulous mind, hesitating though hardly knowing why—or still oftener, perhaps, real indecision as to the propriety of making the final step, are the usual motives for such a refusal. With Joseph Carriere, on the contrary, it came from that strength of character and steady decision of purpose and principle which distinguished him afterwards through life.

The too famous Cardinal Maury was then, nominally, at the head of the diocese of Paris. What right he had to be there was not yet properly known. That he really had none, the prohibitive bulls of the Pope afterwards proved. They had not yet been published, still the young seminarian of St. Sulpice (thanks to what he had been taught) considered himself justified in regarding the position of his Eminence, if not wholly unauthorized, at least not duly canonical. Knowing, therefore, that for the time being he could receive orders from no other prelate than Cardinal Maury, he made no he-

hesitation in declaring that he preferred not to take them at all.

In our days of well-regulated ecclesiastical discipline, it is not easy to appreciate this piece of apparent self-reliance on the part of a mere seminarian But it must be remembered that the circumstances of the time were very peculiar; and, besides, that although no doubt the act tended not a little to compromise M. Carriere personally, the responsibility mainly lay with the seminary, of whose teaching he was naturally supposed to be but an exponent. As we have already remarked, in those days of unsettled ecclesiastical organization and, it must be said, of too frequent clerical weakness in the Church of France, there existed in the healthier portion (and to the honour of the Sulpiceans be it said, nowhere more than with them) a spirit of Catholic independence amounting to positive distrust of local ecclesiastical superiors when known to be not "on good terms with Rome." Those who in a proper state of things should think only of obeying immediate authority, were obliged to think for themselves, and often with some difficulty to form their consciences before acting. A great evil this is, to be sure, and in the Catholic Church must be regarded as a highly abnormal state of things; but history has shown it of not unfrequent occurrence, and our own troubles about the " Veto" present for it abundant analogies. That

M. Carriere was right in the particular case alluded to, the subsequent publication of the Papal bulls forbidding Cardinal Maury *any act of administration* has established beyond doubt. His refusal therefore of orders from the hands of one so exalted in the Church of France, and so favoured by the state, as the reputed archbishop of Paris, must be taken in the light it always has been regarded, as a trait as honourable to himself as it is creditable to his college.

For, while giving the young student full credit for all the firmness of character and adhesion to principle which his act entitles him to, we must remember that the honour reflects on the house which nourished the spirit it betrayed, and which, of course, remained responsible for the result.

In doing so, however, it is evident from what we have already said, St. Sulpice only acted up to the professed spirit of its traditions, and in accordance with the line of conduct it had hitherto pursued during the trying circumstances of the period.

M. Carriere had long entertained the thought of joining the Sulpiceans. Their fidelity to the Church, as well as to the professed principles and rules of their body, during the general break-up of the great Revolution—their traditional adhesion to the centre of Catholic unity, and the name they had won for unsullied purity of faith, especially during the fearful doctrinal epidemic of Jansenism—when, according to Fenelon,* almost all other religious bodies in France were more or less infected but theirs—these, and other not less pleasing features of the community founded by Monsieur Olier, offered so many guarantees in those dangerous times highly attractive for a young man who felt himself called to a life of study and religion. The more intimate knowledge of the rules and the general working of the society, and the closer acquaintance with the lives of its members which his stay in the college afforded, soon ripened his former intention into a decided resolve, and before the completion of his course he applied for admission. The then superior-general, M. Duclaux, had known his young postulant only to love and admire him, and was of course but too happy to receive him amongst the ecclesiastics over whom he presided.

At the time we write of, the Church of France (with that inextinguishable vitality inherent in every member of Christ's mystic body) was fast recovering from the seeming death-blow given it by the late Revolution. The religious family throughout the country of course grew apace in size and importance, and the work of its nursery, St. Sulpice, increased in proportion. Amongst other houses of the company, the seminary of Paris, though

* See Rohrbacher, Hist. Ecclesiast.; art. Jansenism.

admitting only theologians and affording accommodation for hundreds, no longer sufficed to contain all the students that from every diocese of France sought for admission. It was therefore found necessary to open a supplementary course of theology in the junior house of Issy (outside the city walls), which had hitherto been exclusively consecrated to the preparatory studies of philosophy and the natural sciences. This highly important chair was conferred on M. Carriere, who, it must be remembered, had but barely completed his own theological studies. As was expected, the distinguished student immediately rose into the distinguished professor. The one, to be sure, does not necessarily follow upon the other; for a learned and talented man may prove a very indifferent teacher. But besides the guarantee which his unusually brilliant course in the seminary at Paris afforded, as we have already seen, he had long before, when teaching at Amiens, although then little more than a boy, given proof of possessing in a very high degree the rare tact of communicating knowledge— and better still, of giving each point a permanent as well as a dictinct, well-defined place in the mind. Even amongst good professors some excell in explaining, some in proving, and others, perhaps, only in "answering objections;" our *beau-ideal* of excellence lies in the happy reunion of the three.

Yet one of the most learned French bishops of the present day, who was at the time in a way to appreciate the lessons of the young professor at Issy has thought fit to say of them, that he never since heard lectures in which a clear exposition of the point at issue, with its various bearings and difficulties, was allied to decisions so well-defined and so satisfactory to the hearers in their logical deduction from the premises or principles given.* A professor of theology thus already distinguished, Joseph Carriere was in orders only a deacon. *He was still too young to be ordained priest.*

So truly (and so beautifully because so truly) has the great poet, Corneille, remarked,

"Dans les ames bien nées
Lâge n' attend point le nombre des années."

Certainly he had not yet completed the number of years required by the canons for the reception of the holy order of priesthood; but in his case applies the poet's remark; for all intents and purposes he was already *old* enough—and so judged his superiors, they who were best able to judge in the matter. Dispensation of age was accordingly applied for, which being granted, and the rescript (as a particular mark of esteem) signed by the Holy Father himself, M. Carriere was ordained priest on the 20th of October, 1817.

* See the notice by l'Abbé Lamazou in the *Journal des Villes et Campagnes.*

CHAPTER III.

M. CARRIERE'S SUCCESSFUL CAREER AS PROFESSOR AND AUTHOR.—CENSURE PRONOUNCED BY THE HOLY SEE ON SOME PROPOSITIONS CONTAINED IN HIS WRITINGS.—CORRECTED EDITION IN CONSEQUENCE.

A COMMON reproach made to the life of religious obedience, as found in all Catholic communities, is the ill effect it is said to have upon the growth and development of the intellectual man. Subjecting one soul to the decisions of another, both as to daily, continual action and occasional production, as to its internal working and the fruits it may bring forth; habituating the mind to disregard the prompting of genius and the instincts of taste, and always to look for orders before acting, or, when its activity has been called forth, to content itself with doing simply its allotted work as best it may, religious obedience is said to cramp thought, to kill intellectual energy, and, by depriving the soul of its native elasticity and self-reliance, to keep down rising genius, to make the mind, not as God made it, a free, self-inspired agent, ready to create; and powerful to execute; but a poor, willing slave, simply capable of doing what is "given unto it to do."

All this is very specious, and very unfair. It is

nothing more or less than the old plan of the adversaries of the Catholic name—to put up for show a system of their own fabrication, and then triumphantly to overthrow it, while taunting the Catholic one with its weakness and defects, and in proof pointing to the ruins of their own.

One can well conceive a system of obedience working precisely in the way above exposed, but it would be as different from that real system peculiar to Catholic communities, as the obedience of a soldier to some stupid, reckless officer is from that of a dutiful son to a highly intelligent and loving father. Like the latter, the obedience of Catholic communities does not check the intellect in its onward career, but prudently guides it on its way; and far from curbing, will spur it on when needful. It does not even weaken the mind's powers of action, but opens fields of labour that the individual would not have thought of entering, or would not alone have dared to work in. A striking feature of every community is, its trying to make the most of its men. The business of the superior and directors of an order or society is, to turn every member to the best possible account; by close and persevering attention to the peculiar talents and tastes of each one, to adapt the work to the man; and once that the right man is in the right place, to give him every opportunity which great experience would advise and, generally, great resources can command, to make the most of his faculties and attainments. Thus, far from being thereby cramped, the result of its life of obedience on the individual mind is, to enable it to develop itself to the utmost, and show itself to the best advantage in that sphere of thought or that field of action which is best suited to the special nature of each one's talents and parts.

It may be said that if this be true, the life of a community under obedience is absolutely the best suited to intellectual growth, as well as to the ripening and saving of the fruits of learning and genius. The consequence, as well as the premise, is we think undeniable, as far at least as ecclesiastics are concerned, and to whom our remarks are confined.

For a proof of the truth of our conclusion, we appeal to the facts, that the highest intellectual achievements in literature, science, and art, which the Church has witnessed within her body, have been accomplished by men living under obedience; and that the vast bulk of published writings—not alone works of piety, but on every species of ecclesiastical lore and learning—does in the present day (as in past ages it always has) come either from out the cloister or from some sort of community with a superior to guide it. To the strengthening influence and saving power of *obedience* the world owes a great deal, but the Church, most of its fruits of literature and learning. Why, then, should it be spoken of as an atmosphere uncongenial to the nature of the human mind, enervating and blighting in its effect, when it has proved itself quite the opposite?

Are there some natures so constituted, that to them obedience in any of its many forms should necessarily prove injurious—men who (independent of divine vocation) are naturally unfit for any of the different orders and societies now to be found in the Church? Likely enough, there are not; for natures of every possible temperament are to be found so placed, and are therein giving evidence of being in their proper sphere. We are now speaking, it must be remembered, only of the effect of obedience on the intellectual faculties; and, regarding it in this light, even if there be some to whom it is not healthful, undoubtedly there are others to whom it is absolutely necessary—souls that would never thrive out of its genial atmosphere—rich minds that would prove barren of fruit but for its fructifying influence; often really powerful intellects that, however, need to be brought out by its attractive power, and require the special support it gives in order to take their proper stand. Such are the souls which the Church most prizes—those in which genius vies with sanctity, talent's restless tendency to "dare deeds of high emprise," and then to exhibit its triumphs, with holy humility's dread of applause, and gentle modesty's instinctive longings to shun all public gaze.

Such a soul was Joseph Carriere's. His was a strong mind, and, as we have seen, he gave early proof of it in the case of his refusal of orders from Cardinal Maury; at the same time, his was an humble soul, and he was a truly modest man. For this reason, although he would have made himself noted under any circumstances of life—for strong talent and sound learning will rise to the surface in some shape or other, no matter what sinking influences contend to keep them down—it is certain that he would have never come out so powerfully as he has done, or in such strong colours, but for living under the fostering care of obedience. Throughout his career, and at every new phase of it, one cannot help being struck by the fact, that he never puts himself forward—he waits to be drawn out, to be brought up to each successive enterprise by his superiors; and, to their credit be it said, right well they acted their part towards him.

The high degree of excellence as theologian and teacher which, as we have related, our young professor evinced while conducting the supplementary course of theology at Issy, marked him out to the attention of his superior as, notwithstanding his youth, capable of filling with honour a still more important chair. He was accordingly, in 1818 (the year after his ordination), called to the chair of Moral Theology in the senior house of St. Sulpice, Paris, where but so lately he was to be seen in the ranks of the students.

Besides the unusually great mass of knowledge he had contrived to amass during his college course, we have seen him in his first chair at Issy give proof of possessing to a very high degree the peculiar qualities required for professing with success. He now displayed, in addition, a peculiar facility in solving difficulties and instantly quashing objections, no matter how specious or well put, which, while it first caused universal surprise, owing to his comparative inexperience, soon became his well-known *forte* and the principal charm of his teaching. Indeed, perhaps, it was this happy facility, more even than the charm of his exposition or the power of his argumentation, that made his "lessons" so famous as they now became throughout France.

Each day now added to his public fame as a professor, to his reputation as a holy priest, and, what perhaps speaks still higher in his favour, to the affectionate regard in which, for his kindly character and genial disposition, he was from the beginning held both by the professors and students. At the same time, the confidence in his virtue and talents already to such an extent, for one of his age, shown him by his superior, also daily increased. Thus, the hopes to which the astonishing success of his first essay in professing at Issy had naturally given rise, were daily more and more fully realized, until, after a short time, he was considered worthy of one of the first, if not of the first, professorship which it was in the power of the company of St. Sulpice, perhaps of the Church of France, to confer on him.

Many of our readers are, no doubt, aware that though not conferring degrees, St. Sulpice is, practically speaking, *the* university of the French clergy, at least in all relating to ecclesiastical sciences. The comparatively deserted Sorbonne enjoys the name, the *grand seminaire* has the reality, and students from every diocese in the country sit in its class-halls, although it is only recognized by the state as the diocesan seminary of Paris.

Besides many secondary advantages calculated to make it preferable to any of the diocesan seminaries of the provinces, a great attraction of this college lies in what is known as *le grand cours de St. Sulpice,* which is a superior or supplementary course of theology, dogmatic and moral, Hebrew, and canon law. This *cours* in many respects reminds one of the Dunboyne establishment of our national college, and is, like it, destined for those who, having completed the usual course of studies, are to remain some time longer in the college. In St. Sulpice, this supplementary course lasts two years. Some follow it because they are preparing for professorships in the seminaries of their respective dioceses; some, because they have been sent to Paris for that purpose by their bishops as a reward for, and a supplement to successful careers spent in their own schools at home; and others, simply because, being of studious habits, they wish to perfect themselves in the different branches of ecclesiastical knowledge, and are privileged by their bishops to remain, in order to avail themselves of the peculiar advantages for that purpose which the *grand cours* affords.

As almost every diocese of France, from time to time, sends a contingent, for the most part of its choicest students, to this superior *cours*, the requirements of any of its professors must needs be of the highest order. Mere acquired learning would never suffice without positive talent; whilst talent, unless furnished with science, rich, varied, and sure, would be worse than useless, for it would be highly dangerous. Moreover, considerable facility being given for discussion, even with the professors, it will be understood how much tact and power of judgment, ready but sure, is necessary to satisfy the queries and meet the objections of such a body of clever young men as these, and who, having fully completed the required course of studies, having to a certain extent ceased to be mere pupils, are disposed and are able to treat their professors like so many discriminating critics. This is especially the case for the class of moral theology, which leaves so much room for discussion, and with whose subject matter the students are already familiar, having studied each question before.

To no one, it would seem, but to some veteran doctor, whose "hair had whitened with the dust of the schools," could such a class be safely entrusted. Yet, whilst the society to which he belonged possessed many venerable ecclesiastics of well-proved ability and learning, the young Abbé Carriere was, after due consideration, the one appointed to fill (of all others) the chair of Moral Theology in the *grand cours*. Thus, when but still a very young man—at an age, indeed, when most men of any profession are still but learning to profit by instruction, or trying to make themselves a name—Joseph Carriere found himself occupying a chair which, in point of honour and importance, was perhaps the highest magisterial seat in the Church of France; not placed there, as many in high positions are wont to be, by influence, intrigue, or the personal efforts of persevering ambition, but duly promoted to it by competent authority, free and unbiassed.

The highest opinion of his powers, and confidence in his success, could alone have overruled the natural objection felt to his age, and raised him to the responsible position he now held; yet never was opinion better founded, never was confidence better placed, for the new professor did all and more than was expected of him.

It is a great treat and a great boon to hear a man of genius speak on any subject or under any circumstances. When, as in the case of our theologian, his subjects are such as are suited to his peculiar talents and tastes, and when he has come prepared to do full justice to them, the pleasure and advantage likely to accrue to the hearers are clearly still further enhanced: when, moreover, like Carriere lecturing to his class, the speaker is in his proper sphere, and addresses an audience that can and does fully appreciate his learning and his powers, the treat is likely to be yet more precious; but when the questions discussed are of great moment, possessing, in addition, a national and contemporaneous interest, such as are those treated in the *grand cours* of St. Sulpice, then, indeed, the hearers may be said to enjoy an opportunity such as seldom falls to one's lot, and which, when it is found, should be availed of to the utmost of one's power. So, no doubt, felt the gentlemen to whom the author of "Justice" and "Contracts" was lecturing; indeed, we have been told that many students of his class used to plead hard with their bishops to be privileged to remain longer than the allotted two years, which is the period fixed by the college regulations.

To give an idea of how fully M. Carriere realized the high hopes entertained of his success, and with what honor to himself, as well as profit to his students, he acquitted himself of the difficult duties of his new charge, it will be sufficient to state that the famous treatises, "*De Matrimonio*," "*De Justitia*," and "*De Contractibus*," are nothing more than part of the lectures delivered from his chair in the *grand cours*.

Of the numbers who are yearly delivering courses of theology, few professors venture to deliver their lectures to publicity; of those who do, still fewer gain any notice unless within a very restricted circle, some not outside their own country, some not outside their order or the college in which they professed. The appearance of Carriere's published lectures has, however, as every Catholic student knows, made a striking page to itself in the annals of modern theological science. His works became almost immediately famous, and are to this day the received class-books with nearly every college in his own country and with many abroad, whilst everywhere known and esteemed, they seldom fail to be referred to when the subjects on which they treat are being discussed, and—most rare privilege for any of the countless religious works continually appearing—are quoted as making considerable authority in the schools, conference-rooms, and other doctrinal assemblies of the Catholic world.

The publication of these volumes was by no means a literary venture, on the contrary, its success was inevitable. Still less was it a literary speculation on the part of Carriere himself; his community desired it, and it was made in obedience to an imperative call from his fellow-clergymen in France, which the author could no longer refuse to comply with. The contents of the "treatises" had become well known to the country through the notebooks of the students of the *grand cours*, turned professors or priests in their respective dioceses; so that their appearance in a printed and authorized form was loudly called for, and, when it did come, was hailed as a national blessing, for, besides their intrinsic advantages as stores of practical information to the general student by their treatment of various theological questions connected with certain enactments of the new "code civil," these works met a want severely felt by French students of moral theology.

As was anticipated, the success of the new *"Theologies"* proved complete and immediate; students, priests, professors, lawyers* even, everywhere read and extolled their contents.

The eldest daughter of the Church is proverbial for making much of her sons. The name of Carriere was accordingly soon on the lips of professors and students throughout the land, when the startling news was spread that his works were condemned at Rome. Great was the general surprise, and, as M. Carriere was already very popular with the clergy of France, who saw in him one of the first stars that began to show in the firmament of their Church darkened over by the late Revolution, great was even the grief of many; great was, therefore, the universal satisfaction when the *dit-on* having toned down to the exact truth, it became known that the censure fell only on one or two of the opinions† upheld in the new works, and which being until then freely taught by most French theologians, the author regarded as still

---

* M. Demante, of the law faculty of Paris, on one occasion jokingly remarked to one of his colleagues of the *Assemblei Constituante*: " Indeed, I think if M. Cremieux had read, as I have, L'Abbe Carriere's treatises on " Justice" and " Contracts," he would be now sorry that he never offered him a president's seat in the *cour de cassation.*" This was in 1848. Such was the high opinion entertained of the works of M. Carriere by the great lawyers of Paris.

† See the notice on Carriere, *Journal des Villes et Compagnes.*

matter of choice dependent on each one's private conviction. Moreover, it was commonly said that the opinions in question were now so much objected to chiefly because of their being supported by an authority otherwise so deserving as, even in the holy city, M. Carriere was considered to be.

No one who knew the modest young Sulpicean, for a moment doubted that his submission would be but what it was, hearty, immediate, and unreserved. A corrected edition of his works was therefore daily expected. Such a one soon appeared, and, having been submitted to the judgment of the Holy See, gave complete satisfaction.

The censures employed by the Church are never vindictive. They are at farthest only corrective, and even for the most part simply curative. So much so, that they are never given, or, if given on trial, cease, when correction is of no avail, or cure is impossible. Moreover, when the object to which they are directly addressed is, as generally happens, rather a thing than a person, they seldom aim at its total destruction, but rather at its greater perfection. Like the Divine Master, the work of holy Church being one of mercy, healing and invigorating is, for the most part, the touch of her hand. So it proved to be in the case before us; for having undergone the purifying action of Rome's examen, and being corrected upon its decision, the now virtually approved treatises were patented sound by supreme authority—indelibly stamped for evermore pure, wholesome food for the Catholic mind.

Nothing more was wanted to ensure their complete success, and college after college began to adopt them as class-books, to be conned over by students, and commented on by learned professors.

Thus the "censure," such as it was, pronounced on M. Carriere's works had the good effect which Rome's strictures should have, meant as they are to "edify," not to destroy, to cure but never to hurt or kill aught that should live. The decision of the Holy See being duly received, while the error it smote was corrected, had a result, even in the author's regard, far from injurious, and made matters ultimately turn out for every party concerned, and in every respect, all for the best. The noise which the censure itself occasioned served to spread Carriere's fame as a remarkable author; his cheerful submission to the judgment of the head of the Church won for him the still more enviable reputation of a right-principled theologian as well as a true-minded priest; and the subsequent "visa" of the Sovereign Pontiff passed on his now authorized writings, like some universal passport, opened to them for evermore undisputed entrance to the Catholic schools of every land; while the Church in

France, naturally most anxious to distinguish herself after her years of silence and abjection, had the great joy of seeing him, whom she had come to regard as her most eminent professor and her greatest living theological author, now taking his stand before the Church at large as one of the first doctors of the age.

It is hard to overrate the intellectual greatness of a man who, at the present day, thus wins for himself a remarkable place in the *legion d'honeur* of Catholic theologians; the more so, when, like our author, his claim to such an honour rests not on mere skilful compilations, manuals, compendiums, and the like; but on really original productions, works which become prized by the learned as books of reference. No field of human science has been so much cultivated as that of Catholic theology. For many centuries, the intellectual might and nearly all the mental energy of the civilized world were wholly given to tilling it in every form and to every possible purpose. Even still, thousands of great intellects are working it, some in one way, some in another. Many centuries ago, none but a powerful and original mind could have succeeded in striking out for itself a new path, or have reaped a fresh harvest of yet unseen fruits in this field of theological labour. What, then, must be said of the mind which contrives to do so now, after that the ground has been seemingly drained of all that it could give out. This much must be said of the writer who has succeeded in adding fresh stores of knowledge, in any shape or in any department, to what already lies stored up in the archives of sacred science (as Joseph Carriere by his three great volumes* has undeniably done), he is more than a great *savant*, or even a great author, he is a truly GREAT MAN.

Arrived at the height of ecclesiastical literary eminence, to which he now saw himself raised, our illustrious Sulpicean, had not yet completed the thirty-third year of his age. An unusual age, the reader will observe, for a man to be regarded by the great and learned of his calling at home and abroad, and approved by the highest authority in his profession, as an oracle of science, and, what still further redounds to his praise, in questions of such vital importance as those touching conscience and the practical rules of morality. Here we pause, for, as we shall explain, we now find our theologian at a turning point of his life—at the end of one career, and at the opening of another.

* We here refer to his large works, of which mere abridgments are used as class-books.

CHAPTER IV.

M. CARRIERE'S MISSION TO AMERICA.—ASSISTS AT THE COUNCIL OF BALTIMORE.—ELECTED SUPERIOR-GENERAL OF HIS SOCIETY.

IF the subject of this memoir had been only a professor or an author, a mere votary of science, we should be content with reviewing his intellectual career, and stopping occasionally to admire the successive triumphs of his genius. But Joseph Carriere was more than a mere literary phenomenon—he was a *priest*, and as such must raise inquiries touching more than his success in professing or writing.

What then, it will be asked, was his general demeanour? what were his dispositions? what, in a word, was his spiritual condition, as externally manifested, all this time? We have seen him pass through a very brilliant career, from honour to honour, entrusted with a succession of highly important charges, each one turned by him into a complete success, until he reached to a height which very few of his profession in the same course ever atttain—and all before he was thirty-three years old. It was enough to turn a young man's head, and materially to injure, if not to spoil, his spiritual state. Joseph Carriere had, however, the happiness of living under obedience,* and had there been any such danger for him, he would not have been exposed to the temptation. There really was none. The young man was gifted with a large fund of common sense, which, being based on Christian principles, and informed by the considerations to which these give rise, as also, no doubt, enlightened and strengthened by constant co-operation with divine grace, effected that, as distinguished student, as rising and then renowned professor, as highly successful author and universally recognised great theologian, M. L'Abbe Carriere's unfailing characteristic remained that of a modest young priest.

We are told that in the chair, even when begining to teach at Issy, his language and manner were quite those of an old professor, betraying little of the tyro's timidity and reserve. It must be remembered, however, that decision of manner and a certain tone of confidence are simply natural to a speaker who has made himself thoroughly master of the subject which he treats, as Carriere invariably did before he sat down to speak to his class. Then should we not say, that whilst teaching the sacred truths of eternal justice, he had good precedent for speaking "like one having authority," without in the least on that account deserving to be regarded as other than

* Although not bound by vow, as his society was only a congregation, not a religious order.

"meek and humble of heart." Moreover, the fact is, that he who in the chair was noticed for speaking in this authoritative manner—like an old master, because he was treating his subjects in true masterly style—was also noticed in chapel and in prayer-hall for his humble mien, and pious, collected bearing, and in recreation was to be distinguished among his companions, priests or students, only by a certain naive simplicity of manner and address, which they who knew him to the last will bear us out in saying, remained even in old age the distinguishing feature of his character.

We thus paused to glance at the moral aspect of M. Carriere's life up to this period of his career, because we had already seen it quite through its intellectual or literary features. The publication of his collected lectures on "Justice," "Contracts," and "Matrimony," which brought that career to so brilliant a climax, was destined to bring it to its close, for his superior decided that those talents, which he had hitherto consecrated to the diffusion of sacred science, had better henceforward be exclusively turned to the direction of that society of which he was a member, and which had the highest claims on his service.

At first sight, one would be tempted to regret that, at the early age of thirty-three, ere the noon of his life, in the full force of his just developed powers, our theologian was taken away from the field of thought which he was apparently still working with such success; at the same time, that there may be reason to wonder how he consented (uncomplainingly as he did) to the change. A first sight is very frequently, as in the present case, not the correct view. Certainly, if Carriere had been a man actuated by motives of ambition or self-interest, it is not likely that he would care to give over professing and writing precisely at the time when the tide of public admiration and confidence seemed full in his favor. His spring of action was not, however, that self-love which the world's selfish philosophy gives as the only one worthy of a sensible man. A priest, the object of his life's labour was to work AD MAJOREM DEI GLORIAM—for that end, and that end only; a Sulpicean, obedience to his superior's decision was for him the safest way of working out the great end of his existence. Every new phase of his career, up to the present, we have seen to have formed itself only in obedience to this call of authority, which was to him the expression of the will of his Father in heaven, and if the present change was made in the same way, was it not as it should be? Beyond all doubt he was right in cheerfully obeying the order he received, and it would be very rash, indeed, to doubt that his superior was equally so in giving it—the more so, that the change was doubtless made with the approval of the directors of his society, for who could pretend to such competent judgment in the matter as they. In his three works on "Justice," "Contracts," and "Matrimony," having treated that special department of theology wherein sacred and civil law, morality and jurisprudence, come to an encounter, Carriere had supplied a want hitherto much felt in his native country. It was his *speciality*, no doubt, also his *forte*, to be able to do so; and that done, they who had best reason to know for what he was suited, considered that his *mission* as an author was over.

The Church in France had good reason to admire in him the qualities of an excellent professor; the Church at large knew and esteemed him for those of an excellent author, original and practical; but his own society had long learned to cherish him for qualities to it, at least, more precious than either of those. Thoroughly imbued with the spirit of St. Sulpice—a perfect Sulpicean—he was found to be gifted with rare administrative powers, joined to a consummate prudence, and great soundness of decision—just the man to aid in directing and governing a community of such wide-spread action as that of the Sulpiceans. It was, therefore, decided that henceforward his talents and energy should be given to serving God more directly than hitherto, through the medium of that religious congregation to which he belonged. It was so decided, simply because it was considered that thus he would be doing more good, and contributing more to the glory of God than if he had been left tilling the field of sacred science and dispensing the fruits of his learned labours.

In 1829, M. L'Abbe Carriere was sent to America, by the then Superior-General of the Sulpiceans, the gentle Monsieur Garnier, on a mission of inquiry into the condition and progress of two very important Sulpicean establishments in that country— the one at Montreal in Canada, the other at Baltimore in the United States. His mission was a highly important one, difficult in many respects, and rather delicate too; for minute inquiries were to be made, negociations entered into, and many binding arrangements agreed on. But our Sulpicean plenipotentiary acquitted himself of his task so as to give full satisfaction to all concerned, and, as was the case in every charge confided to his care, with no small degree of honour to himself. The author of the life of M. Emery,* referring to the establishment of the Society of St. Sulpice in America, finds himself obliged to dwell on the great advantage of M. Carriere's

* M. Gosselin, author of the well known work, " The Power of the Pope in the Middle Ages ;" translated into English by a professor of Maynooth.

visit to both—so much did this visit form an epoch in the history of these institutions; for otherwise the author of L'Abbe Emery's life would not have noticed it, having made a rule throughout his work to refer as little as possible to any of the living members of his society.

Long before Monsieur Carriere came to America, his fame had reached its shores, so that when he arrived there he found himself almost as well known among the clergy of Canada and the States as he was in his native France. As the first Council of Baltimore was about being celebrated at the time of his arrival, he was earnestly invited by the bishops to attend in the capacity of theologian. Acting in such a capacity—a theologian amongst theologians—the great Sulpicean was in his proper element; and he proved it, to the admiration of all, though, it must be added, to the surprise of none of the assembly; for the readiness of conception, maturity yet quickness of decision, accuracy and extent of knowledge which he there displayed, were only what was expected from a doctor of whom all had heard so much. But it appears* that this illustrious meeting of priests and prelates was not a little surprised, and of course proportionally edified, by his unaffected modesty, and that *naive* simplicity of manner which was all his own.

* Monsieur Lamayou, in the "*Journal des Villes et Campagnes,*" already referred to.

Le bon Père Carriere! when we think of him as he was known to us a few years ago—so perfectly natural in all he said and did, so humble in tone and manner with the youngest student of his house, so charmingly simple in every way, and homely in fact—verily, of our own accord we would have said that at no period of his life could he have in aught realized a free Columbian's idea of "one of the most remarkable men of the day;" and taking into account all the good bishops had heard of Carriere of St. Sulpice, we can well conceive the surprise of the Council of Baltimore, on beholding in the famous Sulpicean nothing more pretentious than a very modest young abbé.

On his return to France, M. Carriere was appointed coadjutor to M. Garnier, the superior-general, whom age and increasing infirmities were rendering daily more incapable of going through the onerous offices of his charge. In his new course of duties, M. Carriere was assisted by M. L'Abbé Carbon, subsequently vice-president of the Paris seminary—that "old Père Carbon" of cherished memory to every Irish student who for the last twenty years passed through St. Sulpice—as so indeed he deserved to be, for the old man's tender heart was particularly soft "*du coté des Irlandais;*" and well they knew it, and much they profitted by it for the gaining of such little relaxations and privileges as an Irish nature or an English stomach will instinctively look for under the somewhat uncongenial discipline of a French college. The asking of a desired permission was gladly deferred to such a time as the gentle rule of M. Carbon's vicegerency would temporarily replace the stricter government of the superior-general, while the latter was absent on his periodical visitation; for it was traditional in the English-speaking circles of St. Sulpice, that of all the year round the *Carbonic* era was essentially the kindest in its yield of favours.

M. Garnier being dead, M. Courson was elected general in his place. Under the latter, M. Carriere was entrusted with nearly the same charges that had been confided to him during the presidency of the former. While discharging these duties of direction and administration—while engaged in the functions of chief director, though remaining in the place of a subordinate, like Hildebrand in a higher sphere, he proved how fitted he was to rule as supreme head. Accordingly, M. Courson's promising presidency being cut short by a premature death, Joseph Carriere was, with the unanimous consent of his brethren, and to the great satisfaction of all members of the clergy, elected Superior of St. Sulpice, and General of all the Sulpiceans in France and America, in the year 1850.

CHAPTER V.

M. CARRIERE'S DAILY LIFE, HABITS, AND OCCUPATIONS, AS SUPERIOR OF ST. SULPICE AND GENERAL OF HIS SOCIETY.

In Italy the people style the General of the Jesuits *Il Papa Nero*, the Black Pope, in contradistinction to *the* Pope, whose cassock is white, while that of the great disciple of St. Ignatius is of dark colour. Popular sayings, always more or less quaint, often somewhat extravagant, have generally much sound sense at bottom, and the sense of the present one is, that the head of a religious body, such as the Society of Jesus, has really a wider and greater influence in the Church than any bishop, archbishop, or even cardinal—is, in fact, like a second Pope. Without meaning to attribute to the office of General of the Sulpiceans such importance as would give its possessor any claims to the title of *Le Pape Noir*, we would say that his position is in many respects the most widely influential in the Church of France. Not only is he, like the General of the Jesuits, superior of a congregation of priests of imposing importance in itself as a religious society, but, like the same influential ecclesiastic, he is the head of a great teaching body, of a teaching body, moreover, which, in the

French Church, has a particular importance, as to its care, has been, in a great extent, entrusted the formation of the young ecclesiastical mind of the country, and, as a natural consequence, of the tone of feeling and manner of thinking of that same clerical mind in its maturity : for who forms the student forms the priest, as to all classes of humanity, clerical as well as secular, applies the Scripture truth, that the young man departs not from the way in which he has been trained.

The office, therefore, of General of the Sulpiceans and Superior of St. Sulpice, to which M. Carriere was now raised, was one of the highest importance, and his elevation to it—its responsibility as well as its dignity—lends an interest to his biography which personal attainments or private deserts, however great, could hardly give; moreover, it confers an importance on a certain feature of his history which, but for it, would be of little importance—that is, his daily life, its habits and occupations, and all details illustrative of the same. To those details, then, it will not be amiss to consecrate a special chapter, remembering that we are now dealing with the subject of our memoir more in his official than in his private capacity—speaking rather of the superior of St. Sulpice than of Joseph Carriere, the theologian.

Before entering into the details in question, and

to begin in a business-like manner, let the important point be settled as to "how much a-year" he had in the elevated position he now occupied. The question is easily answered; perhaps the answer will not be so easily believed—he had *nothing;* that is to say, nothing in the way of pounds, shillings, and pence; for it is to be hoped that at the end of each term he had secured for himself a fair stock of merits, and that on his last reckoning-day he found a goodly sum set down to his account in the bank of that realm where he now abides.

"Then he was left want for nothing!" Very few professional men of distinction outside the profession to which he belonged would, we are inclined to think, be content with such a negative salary as that. However; it is true he wanted for nothing; but also, it must be added, in order to attain that enviable state of freedom from want, he had to take the precaution of wanting very little. An humble son of toil—say one of your much pitied labourers of Lancaster—would lay out more on his precious person in a working quarter than the distinguished president of St. Sulpice did, or would have been expected to spend on himself, in a twelve-month. "But his apparel—his wardrobe?" Fancy and fashion had not much to do with it, nor, as a natural consequence, had expense either. A simple soutane, a cincture, and a pair of shoes were the only visible and the principal items of his ordinary dress, to which, for outside costume and walking out, was simply added a common hat, sometimes a plain outside coat; and these articles renewed at certain rather distant periods, although always clean, were often such as to give unmistakeable evidence of the wearer's being a customer of little value to hatter or tailor. "Well, then, what is to be said of his apartments, their furniture, and the various details of their keeping?" Were it question of the dwelling of an Oxonian or Trinitarian clerical professor, or of even a respectable student of either establishment, we should in answer have to speak of chambers or rooms; it being, however question only of the rector of the first ecclesiastical college in France, suffice to mention, that besides his little bed-chamber, the very rev. gentleman had one room—reception-hall, study, sitting-room, all in one—a room which, doubtless, he found furnished just as his predecessor had left it, and, when he himself died, left pretty much in the same way as he found it. No doubt, to a Sulpicean eye that apartment was highly ornamented, decorated as it was with much that was suggestive of evangelical poverty and ecclesiastical simplicity, which, to a Sulpicean mind, constitute the fairest ornaments of clerical life in all its phases. But to the untutored eye of a casual observer, the room was singularly bare—that is to say, bare of such mundane attractions as hangings, carpetting, fine furniture, or ornaments of any kind—presenting much to remind one of the plain cell of a religious (although M. Carriere was not one), but very little that was suggestive of the best apartment of the distinguished rector of a great college; or rather, with its plain walls, paper covered desk, and general business-like appearance, calculated to impress the uninitiated visitor with the idea that he stood in an attorney's office.

"But," the English reader may ask, "as you are entering into such petty details of his way of living, how *did* he live? What of his table and *its* furniture—his *cuisine* and *its* expenses? There is the real touchstone; therein lies the vulnerable point in the private life of Popish ecclesiastics, especially when passed under the fine cloak of religious community?" " The pleasures of the table are the only sensual enjoyments in which their Church allows them free scope," remarks an English wit, with more good nature than good sense, " who will blame them if they turn its *indulgence* to good account, and, revelling in the sweets they can enjoy, make up for the absence of those enjoyments to which they cannot pretend." And this kindly plea for the poor monks, and priests, is only consequent on a pretty general, almost the popular belief, of enlightened England as to the state of monastic existence and of Catholic ecclesiastical life in general—viz., that its days are spent in eating and drinking (with occasional intervals of doing nothing) and its nights in sleeping out the effects of both, for the purpose of being able to begin a renewal of the same monastic exercises on the morrow. Would that the popular mind of this enlightened English public did turn to fairly probing the "sore place in the life of Popish ecclesiastics," or that research's piercing fork, in the hands of popular historians, did it for them: many an old English proverb would be forgotten, many a time-honoured *dictum* would lose its credit, and no few favourite flowers of English poesy, in the light of the new discovery, found rank with lies, would lose their ancient charms. But to *the* point. The rector of the diocesan college of Paris dined and supped with the students in one of the common refectories of the establishment. However, while the professors and directors of the house all sat at the same tables as the students, and amongst them, he, with his vice-rector, enjoyed the privilege of a separate table at the head of the hall. So placed, he was afforded an opportunity of savouring his repast by observing how things in general went on, and seeing that all was right. At the same time, he was understood to be on the *qui vive* for possible omissions, or faults of pronunciation on the part of the young gentleman who read aloud during the time of meals; or if, instead of a book being read, a sermon was preached in the refectory pulpit, as was the case during a certain part of the year, the rector was expected to take such note of everything connected with the sermon, the preacher, and his preaching, that not only a full and correct account of the discourse itself as to matter and form, but a complete and *fair* criticism on its mode of delivery was looked for at his hands, as a matter of course, that evening, by all the students assembled in the prayer-hall for spiritual lecture. In the spiritual phraseology of St. Sulpice, meals (dinner especially) are rather naively styled important *duties;* undoubtedly they were so for the very reverend rector, and rather onerous duties too.

Those who have experienced its wholesome simplicity will agree with us in saying that Sulpicean fare by no means reaches the sumptuous; in fact, goes rather the other way. Then, suffice it to say, that the superior's *table* at every meal differed little in any respect from that of the youngest student in the refectory, except inasmuch as his dishes were in nowise restricted as to quantity—the which distinction, by the way, could be hardly considered an advantage in his case, for very few of the young gentlemen present (except perhaps on the eve of entering the infirmary) thought of restricting themselves to the quantity which satisfied their venerable rector. It remains to be added that outside the common refectory and the time of meals, private feasting, or still less *vinous* refreshments, were never thought of by rector or professors. The rule of the house made no provision for such private indulgence, which rendered it illicit; and the *econome*, or bursar, made none, which rendered it unfeasible. It was not then unadvisedly we observed that very few British sons of toil are to be found labouring throughout merrie England, who do not spend more in "keeping themselves up," than sufficed, and, we may say, suffices, to maintain the first collegiate rector in the church of France.

"But, then, the expenses consequent on his elevated position—his private equipage, for instance, liveries, carriage horses, and so on—did not these amount to something?" His position, certainly, was an elevated one—the highest of its kind in the empire—in reality, the first ecclesiastical presidency in France; and if an Anglican divine held a similar position in the sister kingdom, he would doubtless require equipages and liveried servants, if only as a "turn-out." The superior of St. Sulpice, however, had nothing of the kind; indeed, for mere relaxation, he seldom or never "turned out" at all, except on walk-days, and then he walked; or if sometimes unable to do so, made use of the common college cab. No display was expected from the rector of the diocesan college of Paris, or from ecclesiastics of his position in general in France, no show of any kind beyond a fair display of learning and piety. "How, then, did he appear in public?" With surplice and stole in his place in the choir of the great church of St. Sulpice during the public offices. He was not to be seen in public anywhere else, unless, indeed, in the street, and then he was to be seen, as the writer remembers him, in simple cassock (with the addition, in winter, of a long coat), a book under his arm, and the French priest's hat on his head, walking steadily along, generally on the road which leads to the junior house at Issy, looking neither to the right nor to the left, and seemingly heedless of all surrounding objects, except such as he had an eye after—the familiar form of some student, which was taken immediate note of, and its individuality determined—or some priest passing him on the way, whom, French fashion, he would never fail to salute.

"What is the use of all these details?" the supercilious reader may inquire; "they are all very commonplace and simple." Very simple, indeed, we confess; but very simple, as a consequence, was the life they reveal, and so we give them, for our task is not to paint or gild that life over, but simply to sketch it as it was in all its simple reality.

Granted, moreover, that there was nothing very peculiar in what we have shown of it, very little even that was particular to Carriere himself. Its details have all the more general interest as giving an insight into the life of a class—not of Carriere alone, but of the superior of St. Sulpice, and, with little difference, of the superiors of all the clerical colleges of France—lives that, however in other respects they may differ, are all alike in this their common feature of simplicity. We might even go outside France, and, inspecting great ecclesiastical institutions of other Catholic countries, have the same to say of their head directors or presidents. Were we, for instance, to do for the distinguished ecclesiastic who bears the proud title of rector of the university of Rome as we are doing for the late superior of St. Sulpice, we should expose a life even simpler still, for we would be detailing that of a simple religious, while M. Carriere was, it must be remembered, a secular priest.

And, as we referred above to the *Black Pope*, it is only fair to add, that the mighty potentate so styled is in reality but an humble priest, who may be daily seen, in the plain habit of an ordinary Jesuit, trudging his way through the streets of Rome (seat and centre of his power though it be), and who, inside his royal home, the Gesu, leads the life of a simple religious, differing in little, except in its greater responsibility, from that of the humblest son of St. Ignatius.

" Well, then," an Anglican reader may still object (should these pages fall under the eye of any such), " this much must be said of the manner of life you have detailed, it is an ungentlemanlike way of living for a man of this Carriere's position in society." It may not be very gentlemanlike in the sense in which the world, especially the English world, mostly takes that word, but it is very ecclesiastical, and to the eyes of the Catholic Church that is everything in the life and habits of a priest, regular or secular, in college or on the mission. Your clerical gentlemen of Oxford and Cambridge rearing, look more to the " respectable;" and, it must be confessed, that in general their " ways" of living are much more calculated to gain the world's respect than those of their clerical counterparts in Catholic countries. But, *que voulez vous*, dear reader, things must be taken as they are. The doctrines and systems of both differ ; so should their ways also, or, if you will, their respective notions of respectability. *De gustibus non disputandum*—or, which comes to the same, each one to the way he thinks best. Those simple-living divines of Catholic countries whom English critics do pronounce in appearance, not respectable, in manner of living, not gentlemanlike, are nothing more nor less than members of that class of men "whose ways are not the world's ways—and, *entre nous,* there is a something in that same which does not speak ill for the religious system of the said divines, or for the nature of the body to which they belong.

In the good old scholastic times, when learning and its dignitaries were duly honoured, some high-sounding or euphonious title was sure to be found for the names of illustrious rectors and great doctors—many of the former had the title by right of succession. Now, by a two-fold claim, our great rector and doctor, Joseph Carriere, is entitled to some such honourable appendage; it is a pity that his name should be left without one. In default of any other, be it the duty of his humble biographer to suggest, CARRIERE RECTOR SIMPLICISSIMUS. You laugh, dear reader; the title is, perhaps, too well deserved to be complimentary; but is it not, think you, right honourable withal? To worldly ears, we know, it will sound far otherwise; but again, we can only say, like people's notions, tastes will differ. Then hear: "The Lord said to him (the demon), Have you considered my servant Job, that there is not his like on earth, *a simple* and upright man? (*Job,* i. 8).—*Qui potest capere capiut.*

Even at the risk of still further showing up our learned rector as a simple man, and perhaps of gaining a like qualification for his poor biographer, we will proceed with the simple details of his daily life. The achievements and great events of a man's life serve to make known his career; a knowledge of his every day life makes known the man.

M. Carriere rose with the community of his college every morning at five o'clock, winter and summer; and, even to the last, was so regular at the morning's first exercises of devotion, that his absence from them was regarded as equivalent to absence from the house. The daily meditation, always of an hour's duration, being over, his was the duty of celebrating mass for the general body of the students. After mass he was again seen kneeling in the chapel, dressed in surplice (as is the custom of St. Sulpice), for his long act of thanksgiving. Having retired to his room, he invariably spent a half-hour in the study of holy Scripture. Not that during the day he did not often spend much more time in the same study, but this half-hour's Scripture in the morning is regarded in St. Sulpice more as a duty taught by the rule than merely an advisable practice, to be recommended for its spiritual advantages. In this, as in other respects, no student observed better the general rules of the house than the superior himself, who was, and seemed called on to show himself, a very model of strict observance. He took care to be present at all the public devotional exercises of the students. At mid-day he gave out the Rosary, and presided at the spiritual reading in the evening, as also at night prayers. These exercises, it will be remarked, together with the recitation of his breviary and the performance of his private devotions, must have taken up a great portion of his day. Yet his duties were many and onerous; but it is incredible how much may be daily done by a strict and well-ordered regulation of time.

"What," it may be asked, "were his duties; and how, as to business, was his day spent?" Treating of any man's life, such a question would be difficult to answer; it is doubly so in the case of one whose duties were necessarily so numerous and so complicated as Carriere's must have been. They were the duties of the immediate superior of the diocesan college of St. Sulpice, Paris, with its 300 theologians, of the Superior-General of all the Sulpiceans in the world, and, as such, of head director of their establishments in America and Canada, and of general inspector of their numerous colleges throughout France (as to the latter, he took care to make himself particularly acquainted with their minutest details by periodical personal visits to each one of them). Then, besides the business consequent on his official duties, being an acknowledged oracle of ecclesiastical science in the Church of France, the friend and confidant of a very large number of its clergy throughout the country, his private correspondence must have been such as would tempt an American editor (proverbially the most belaboured of his class) to throw up his place in disgust. " How Carriere used to spend his time, indeed !" the wonder was with many who knew him, how he spent it as he did, and was not spent out himself long ago, but was, instead, always hale and hearty. A detailed account of the amount of active mental occupation (including devotional exercises) daily persevered in through life by the superior of St. Sulpice and men of his class, would seem simply incredible to one not acquainted with the facilities for purely intellectual labour possessed by members of the Catholic priesthood, especially by those who live in community; it would hardly be credited even by a Catholic who does not happen to know the actual working of such a life, and who, therefore, has no idea of the wonders, in the way of active employment, which may be worked by great religious zeal on the one hand, and strict discipline, with a well ordered distribution of time, on the other. To take for example the case before us. Carriere was not only free from those business and family solicitudes which perplex laymen, but was quite undisturbed by any of these many secular cares which so distract and divide the attention of secular priests, for his *econome* or bursar saw to all such things, and left him to the purely spiritual and intellectual occupations of his office. The man was thus enabled to give himself, heart and soul, completely up to the duties of his charge, while a set rule of life for each day (one which was the result of much experience), and a strict regulation of time, with just enough for rest and mental relaxation to keep the mind in good working order, enabled him to turn to full account the great opportunities he enjoyed for complete self-devotion to his duties.

M. Carriere was happily gifted with much natural energy of mind and body. Age brought with it, although few infirmities, considerable diminution of physical energy; his mental activity, however, seemed only to increase with his advancing years; perhaps because, with the consciousness of life's approaching end, the value of time was being more fully realized; and certainly towards the end of his life this became a favourite subject for his discourses. For the several years during which we knew him (and, as we could hear, it was so long before) the old superior of St. Sulpice seemed to have no regular mental relaxation at all, except the time allotted by the rule for sleep. Every day, after meals, he used regularly repair to his study, and during recreation time we frequently found him at his work-table. Then, the college vacation he invariably passed inside, at the junior house of Issy, where, as we remember (for we had the happiness of staying three months with him in that quiet abode) his time was mostly spent between the chapel and his study. Indeed, for him vacation seemed rather a period of studious retreat than one of holiday enjoyment, rather a change of occupation than a respite from labour. Recreation, as such, he never seemed to take in any form, unless when it came in the discharge of his duties.*

* As a keen appreciation of the advantages of recreation is a feature of collegiate philosophy everywhere, a problem often discussed among the students of St. Sulpice, in our time, was how the Superior could reconcile this apparently total absence of recreation with his conscience, or with his well-known sound principles of life and action. Many theories used to be advanced for the solution of the difficulty. The best received, and propably the right one, was that, to all intents and purposes, he actually did take recreation sufficient for his wants ; but that, in order to economize time, he so contrived to arrange his various occupations, that, whilst always usefully employed, *aliquid utilitatis pro communi laborans*, one kind of business served by its variety in guise of recreation to another, and that as for the vacation "run"— the indispensable supplement to the scholastic year, the only efficient duster of the collected dust of schools—he made up for its loss by his annual visits of inspection to the various houses of his society throughout France. Every theory must needs be opposed, and to this it would be objected that it were just as unreasonable to regard a bishop's visitation of his diocese as *his* relief from pastoral duties, which would certainly be rather unfair. We read, however, of a French bishop who regarded his visitation in this light, but it must be added he was of an extraordinary supernatural turn. When once asked to repose a little from his continued labour, he replied: "Once my eternity begins, I shall have

So that it used to be said of him, that if no one else in the world, at the present day, thought of doing so, *he* carried out to the letter Thomas à Kempis' rather difficult prescription for the life of a good religious (book i., chap. 19) : "*Nunquam otiosus, sed semper aut legens, aut scribens, aut meditans, aut orans, aut aliquid utilitatis pro communi laborans.*" So passed, M. Carriere's days may indeed be called "full;" and in his case, at least, one has no difficulty in conceiving the practicability of rendering the threatened strict account of even every *idle* word.

Well may Socialists exclaim, in view of lives such as Joseph Carriere's: "No wonder for the

time enough to repose." This reminds us of another theory for the solution of the Carriere difficulty; rather of the transcendental order, it found favour in the high-ascetic circles of the college, and was to the effect that the holy man sought no longer for recreation here, but looked for it (like the bishop above cited) to heaven's only true enjoyment and repose; and as for vacation, that he waited for the end of life's year of toil, for the "breaking up" of its business and its cares, until with death should begin his eternal holiday among the blest. But *en attendant?* Well, it was suggested, that in his case, superabundant fortifying grace made up for the natural requirements of an ordinary mortal. There are very few questions on which doctors will not differ, and very many which when fairly exposed, with their *pro's* and *con's*, lead to no more certain conclusion than *discrepant doctores*. Is it so with the above exposition of the Carriere question? Even if so, this much comes of it for certain, the students of St. Sulpice entertained a high opinion of their old Superior, and of the use he made of his time.

Church of Rome to be unconquerable when she has such devoted soldiers to fight her battles; no wonder for her work in society to hold on and prosper, still, in spite of the opposition of intellect, passion, and power, when she has such servants consuming themselves all day long in her service." But we may ask, do these men make the Church? or is it not rather the Church that makes them?— She who *was* before Carriere or those like him ever were. Since, then, philosophers, this preternatural discipline of the soldiers of our Church so excites your wonder, since the self-devotion of her sons demands your admiration, give "honour where honour's due"—to the Royal Mistress who gathers these volunteers together—to the Mother who brings forth and rears these sons, teaching them to do her arduous work so well, and charming them into doing it, alone of soldiers, alone of workmen in the world, not for money's *pay*, but all for LOVE.

Besides perfect employment of time and complete devotion of self to the interests of the Most High, the manner of life adopted by M. Carriere, and, in general, by men of his position in the Church, displays a certain feature, which cannot fail to impress with its consequences any thinking observer. We refer to the peculiar advantages it presents for the preservation and perfect action of all the mental faculties. Is it not evident that a life, such as the one in question—of day by day attention to intellectual and spiritual things—an attention neither interrupted by household anxieties, family solicitude, or secular cares, nor disturbed by the dissipation of pleasure, nor even weakened by the occasional distractions of social enjoyments, together with early rising, regular hours, and general simplicity of living, should necessarily have the effect of *spiritualizing* the whole being, in the most intellectual sense of that word, of purifying the heart, cooling, clearing, and maturing the judgment, and ultimately turning out (as far as the individual is capable of it) a right-minded man— one who may be expected to perceive clearly and appreciate justly what comes under his consideration? In this purely intellectual aspect, the manner of life peculiar to M. Carriere, and to Catholic doctors in general, seems to us to stand in striking contrast to that of the rest of the world beside; not merely of the family-burthened clergymen of Protestant communions, but of all classes of men of the world; and, as it is without parallel in any other sphere of existence, to be without equal in its intellectual and spiritual advantages. Certainly, the manner of life common to men of the world, by the very points in which it differs from that of our religious and collegiate communites, is much better calculated to teach worldly wisdom, as it affords in a much greater degree that acquaintance with the ways of human passion and the tricks of human deceit which is called "knowing the world." But for what remains within the limits of thought, and even of legitimate observation, for the clear perception of philosophical and religious truths, with their necessary relations to one another and to society, the life peculiar to our colleges and cloisters is incomparably better adapted. It may not be the sort of thing to turn out " a clever man of the world," but it is the sort of thing to secure what it is meant to effect, a good churchman, one whose heart is pure, but stocked with true and noble sentiments, and whose head is clear of evil knowledge, but well furnished with all that it is well for it to contain—a man formed after the great apostle's prescription, " Simple in evil, but wise in good."

Now it is well to bear in mind that the kind of life whose singularly favourable opportunities in the intellectual and spiritual order we here expose, not only is that of the men who, like M. Carriere, are charged with forming the rising generation of Catholic clergy throughout the Church, but is, with all its advantages, that of the men who, under the Captain's eye, are at the helm steering the bark of Peter.*

* See the view Cardinal Wiseman gives, in his " Last Four Popes," of the daily life of the Roman ecclesiastics who form the Papal court and constitute the Pontifical congregations. The members of those " congregations," or, as we should say, boards, are professors of eminence or learned religious.

Moreover, it should be remembered that such is not only the life of those who, in their individual capacity as private doctors and approved theological writers, are the ordinary exponents of Catholic doctrine and the credited compilers of codes of Catholic morality, but that it is the life of the men who are behind the scenes in all the great acts and public manifestations of the Church before the world—of those doctors who, either in Rome itself or at a distance from it, and from one another, in different abodes of clerical learning throughout the world, share in the production of even the official anouncements of the Church's will, such as her decrees, her constitutions, or her still more solemn encyclicals—productions of which the authorship is much more general than is commonly imagined, and which, if viewed only in a scientific or literary light, as many of our English critics only regard them, should be taken, not as the works of any individual or even of a clique, but as the authentic expressions of the Catholic mind, with Rome's seal upon them to guarantee their authenticity. Were this fact duly realized, it appears to us that critics hostile to the Church would, in common fairness, treat her solemn decisions with more respect, and unreflecting Catholics would lose much of that diffidence with which they are sometimes found to regard them.

Your scribbling journalist, who has not given a year

of his life, perhaps not a day, to the regular study
of philosophical or religious truth, will deem himself
competent to sit in judgment on these solemn declarations, although he knows them to be those of an
authority, which, in spiritual matters, is the highest
in the world; aye, and if you believe him, in the might
of his superior knowledge and ability, to overthrow
those laboured monuments of learning and reflection.
Forsooth, in the pure atmosphere of thought wherein a London newspaper writer spends his learned
existence, the truths of philosophy and religion must
needs appear clearer far, than in the intellectual
mist and haze through which is passed the life of
your college and cloister-confined doctors of the
Church of Rome. The tranquillizing effects of
family cares and money-making pursuits, the studious influences of theatre, club, and pleasant social
parties, not to speak of taverns and cigar divans,
have toned down his soul into a deeper state of reflection than the said doctors may ever hope to reach;
so that this untaught teacher of the people can at a
glance see the fallacy of the conclusions at which
these legions of doctors and hoary sages have
arrived, perhaps after years of reflection and mutual
consultation; and without the least suspicion of
presumption on his part, will condemn their decisions as "intolerably absurd," "outraging the
first principles of reason and common sense," and

so on.* What the man thus condemns is Catholic, and, therefore, the greater part of the English public will applaud his sentence; but also, because it is unworldly, certain Catholics will naturally be found half inclined to do the same. There are those, however, who will think before they applaud; and who, in judging between the Church and her adversaries, even before entering into the merits of their respective causes, and without going to any transcendental considerations, will ask their common sense, which of the two, the Catholic doctors of Christendom, or their English critics of a London newspaper office, are most likely to think unreasonably, to judge rashly, or to speak unadvisedly, on questions of philosophical and religious truth; there are those, we say, who can discriminate between lives of meditation, silence, regularity, and habits of interior recollection, on the one hand, and lives of continual distractions and frequent dissipation, on the other; between a life-long course of regular study, and occasional application to unguided random reading; between the authors and editors of a Papal Encyclical, and the men who criticize and condemn it, as to the guarantees they separately offer in their lives, for clearness of perception, purity of appreciation, and maturity of judgment.

* By several of the leading organs of opinion in England the late Encyclical has been thus qualified.

Multifarious and onerous as we have shown M. Carriere's duties to have been, exact and strict as were his own habits of life and the order of his daily actions, he was not, as might be expected, in the least morose, stiff, or austere to others, and though by acquirements, by fame as well as by position, he stood on a very lofty eminence, he was by no means inaccessible, or at all sequestered in his greatness—quite the contrary. Not only was he the spiritual adviser of many young clergymen of Paris, but he was also the confidant in private missionary difficulties, and affairs of conscience, of numerous priests in town and country throughout France, and even in foreign lands. We have already spoken of the ease with which he lent himself to correspondence with priests on the mission. That no letter from them was ever left unanswered, might be said to be only part of his well regulated habits of life; but that any communication addressed to him by the most obscure parish priest, or the youngest curate entering on the mission, should invariably meet with a ready and satisfactory reply, accompanied, if ever he had known the writer, with some token of affectionate recollection and a word of encouragement—as in the French journals, after his death, several testified to be the case—this surely was due to something more attractive in a man's character than merely a well-disciplined mind. If thus obliging to those who stood in no immediate relation to him, it need hardly be said that he was uniformly affectionate and open to all directly under his charge. He had a kind look and a pleasant word for everyone, so that the most timid freshman of the college would not have had the slightest hesitation in "making up to him" in corridor or cloister. Those who have had any experience of St. Sulpice are aware that, in M. Carriere's time (unless he happened to be particularly engaged), M. le Superieur's room was always understood to be open to any, even the youngest of the students, who might come and sit there for no other purpose than to have doubts removed or scruples allayed; aye, or even only to seek spiritual consolation or encouragement, in accordance with that beautiful system of "*direction*" which, with the free communication it opens between professors and students, is one of the characteristic charms of this holy house. To ease a burthened heart, to restore peace to a troubled soul, or decision to a wavering mind were privileges which the old superior was known to court. The asking of a permission would be often availed of by him to bring out an exposure of some hidden cause of unhappiness, some secret soul-sore, whose external symptoms had caught the keen eye, and soon disappeared, with their cause, before the skill of this great doctor of souls.

Indeed, no student ever passed through the college who did not at some time or other, as many very often did during their course, share with him such intimate and confidential relations. Not having yet done so, not having (as the saying was) yet made *sa petite histoire à M. le Superieur*, was equivalent to not having yet been duly initiated. Our own most pleasing, as they are most vivid reminiscences of Monsieur Carriere are from *entretiens* such as these.

CHAPTER VI.

FRANCE AND ROME—QUESTIONS ABOUT M. CARRIERE'S SENTIMENTS IN CONNEXION WITH BOTH.

FRANCE is undeniably a great nation, great in all that may constitute a nation's greatness. If, in some respects, her people have a superior, in most, it has no equal. On whatever course it takes, that mighty nation will force itself into the van; it must lead the way, or help to guide, when it may not absolutely command. First in the social, to a certain extent first in the intellectual, and certainly first in the political world—in ruling the destinies of nations; it would be also first in the religious world—in guiding the eternal destinies of man, but that heaven's decree is in its way; as it may not sit on the first seat, it stands in the foremost place. Incarnate Omnipotence has made Rome sole mistress and mother of His Church. France has won the proud title of her Eldest Daughter, for centuries having borne its responsibility, and long and nobly having done its duties. Even now, sadly weakened and sorely lacerated as she is by social evils, still true to her post of honour, she can boast that of all the work done in her mother's house, her's remains the largest share, as it should be, the eldest's portion. Then lately, when Mother Rome spoke that order, which, ringing with the old thunders of the Vatican, was, in its expression as much as in its nature, calculated to sound so harshly on the world's ears, of all the sister churches, whose voice but that of the eldest, the voice of the Church of France! was heard loudest and clearest re-echoing her mother's orders? We cannot praise her power and filial devotion without paying our tribute to her beauty, as well we may, for, save and except the local Church of Rome itself, the "holy place" of the "holy city," no church, all Christendom over, can boast of such a sanctuary as that Church of France. As pure there may be (so we trust is our own), but none is there so redolent of the true odour of priestly sanctity, ecclesiastical spirit, and apostolic zeal.* Why should we be shy of ad-

* That the unenviable reputation under which the French clergy laboured some time ago, in the days of a Maury or a Talleyrand, was in reality undeserved, the very flourishing condition of their body at present may prove without any further investigation; for though individuals may, a diseased *body* of men does not right itself so suddenly, and with such little signs of great interior reformation. We know that the clerical body of France was then healthy and pure, because it is so perfect now. The corrupt lights, which for its own ends secular power, by stealth or open force, had placed in the sanctuary, shed a false, lurid glare upon the whole, and made it look far other than it really was. All such lights are now extinguished, and the sanctuary of the Church in France, appearing in its true colours, is seen to be bright indeed, in reality

mitting all this? Far be it from the Church of Ireland to feel jealous of her sister's superiority. Were the child of St. Patrick as powerful as the great daughter of St. Denis, she would, we know, be quite as efficient, for she has proved, in the least, fully as devoted; moreover, had she had the same opportunities of self-perfection, she would, we believe, have proved just as fair to look on, and we trust the day is not far distant when she shall be seen so. No, far be it from us to feel in aught jealous of our eldest sister; with a family pride we are proud of her beauty; we but feel more powerful in her power; and do heartily glory in her glories, for all goes to the greater honour of our common mother, to the greater good of our common house on earth, and the greater glory of our common Father in heaven.

But of all that is human, or in its nature contains a human element—save of that one Being in whom humanity, united to perfection itself, hath become perfect—admiration must be qualified; so, in consequence, must be praise; and we have a fault to find with this fair Church of France. Our eldest sister makes too much of herself in her mother's house. This may be considered a very pardonable failing, seeing that she really is for so much there, but its cause does not come from the greatness of her ser-

a "holy place," with a clergy such as the priesthood of the New Law should be, "a pure nation, and a most holy race."

vices; that belongs to her better nature, that comes of her virtue, and would never produce the evil result we deplore; its source lies in her grosser nature, in her human element, and it is overweening nationalism.

Now, we are far from blaming nationalism in individual priests, for so individualized, we can regard it as nothing less than the concrete form of the abstract virtue of patriotism, that virtue which the divine Spirit himself has deigned to illustrate for our greater admiration in one of the most touchingly beautiful pictures of the Gospel page—the one wherein the Man-God is seen pensively looking down upon his own Jerusalem, God, thinking of the torrents of wrath which of his justice he was about to pour on the devoted capital; Man, of the tenderness of his loving nature, out of the fulness of his human heart, weeping for the hapless lot of the land that gave him birth.* Mindful of that patriot Priest of Priests, that Incarnate God in tears for the future woes of fatherland, how can

* *Luke*, xix. 41, 43 : " And when he drew near, seeing the city, he wept over it," not only for its spiritual evils, but for its impending political and social misfortunes, as the Gospel explains : "He wept over it, saying: If thou hadst known, and that in this thy day, the things that are to thy peace: but now they are hidden from thy eyes. For the days shall come upon thee, and thy enemies shall cast a trench about thee, and straighten thee on every side : and beat thee flat to the ground, and thy children who are in thee : and they shall not leave in thee a stone upon a stone."

we blame, how can we but admire patriotism or nationalism even in priests? And we do not blame, and we do admire it in them when it is in its proper place. By all means, a clergyman should stand up for his nationality, and love to show himself under its distinctive colours; for besides his official capacity as a priest, in his private capacity as a man, as well as any of his fellow-countrymen, he is a son of fatherland. But the clerical body of a country has no such double capacity, it is simply a division of the servants of the Catholic sanctuary—a portion of the undivided clerical body of the Catholic Church. What right, then, has a clergy to put itself forward as anything more than Catholic, to hold on to peculiarities, or stand up for privileges, beyond what that general privilege supposes, or even to boast of a more distinctive title than that of Catholic, unless, indeed it be that of its patriarchate, as those of the Western Church may call themselves Roman. Inside the Church as there is no distinction of Jew or Gentile, there should be none of English, French, or Irish; within her sacred precincts nothing connected with the trifles of this passing life should be noticed; and such is nationality at best, a thing of earth, which if exhibited in the temple, being not of the temple, is simply out of place: a man may as well bring in the implements of his trade, and make a show of them before the altar. But within the sanctuary itself, nationalism is not only an intrusion, it is an intolerable nuisance. It mystifies simple orders, and canons of universal application, it complicates rubrics, spreads general confusion, and, by spoiling the harmony of its different parts, strangely disturbs the beautiful order of the whole. An Irish priest wishing to celebrate in vestments green shamrocked all over, or a French one appearing at the altar in a chasuble of the national tricolour, instead of the colour of the day, while it may illustrate the incongruity, shows the absurd tendency of nationalism working within the sanctuary. Now, the otherwise faultless clergy of France must be blamed for its peculiar bearing towards this abuse. Of all the reproaches which history has to address to that glorious body, this *petite misere* of misplaced nationalism is the root and centre. The French ecclesiastical plague of peculiar liturgies and diocesan breviaries was generated by it; Gallicanism is simply synonymous with it; so is Parliamentism (to coin a word); and history says that Jansenism, if not directly sprung from either, was nursed by these both. Then, at the present day, that *je ne sais quoi* which so unfavourably distinguishes a certain class of the French clergy (and of which we shall speak anon, but which we may now designate as a want of cordiality towards Rome), is after all but a weed of the same nationalistic seed—

a suckling of buried Gallicanism, which, for their own purposes, secular power and secular literature carefully foster. The consequence of this sinister peculiarity of the Church in France is, that certain suspicions hang always about its remarkable members, so that questions of a certain import must be answered by the biographer of a French theologian or a French ecclesiastical dignitary, which would not be thought of in connexion with almost any other churchman.

The biographer of the late Superior of St. Sulpice must, therefore, take upon himself to ask and answer such questions in his regard. Then, in the first place, " Was Joseph Carriere a Gallican ?"

A century ago (or less), such a question could have received an immediate and direct reply—a simple affirmative or negative. Not so now, it can only be answered, Irish fashion, by putting another : " What does the question signify ?" In what sense is the word Gallican taken ? For there is Gallicanism, a French system of doctrine opposed to the infallibility of the Head of the Church, and Gallicanism, which only means a class of French sympathies inimical to certain Papal prerogatives of ecclesiastical discipline. If the question be understood in the first sense, our answer simply is, Carriere was not a Gallican. The doctrine whose votaries are branded with that now somewhat odious epithet, must be, and is regarded by modern theologians as, though not heretical, pretty evidently *erroneous.* Such a doctrine the late superior of St. Sulpice was, it need hardly be said, too sound a doctor to adopt. It is certain that he never taught it. Indeed, doctrinal Gallicanism may be said to exist no longer, even among the clergy of France: at least, it does not venture to show itself, which practically comes to the same. It is not defended in places which were considered its stronghold; and it is unnecessary to state that it has not found a refuge in the college over which M. Carriere presided, for it never took a hold there.

It is much easier to change the head than the heart; and often where convictions are renounced, accompanying sympathies are retained. Although by force of argument, Gallicanism in doctrine has been rooted out of the clerical mind in France, a certain tone of feeling really Gallican does exist in certain portions of it, though to a very limited extent.

As the characteristics of this sympathetic Gallicanism, may be given, intense devotion to France, and unbounded admiration of everything French, with a corresponding jealousy of Rome, joined to a sort of instinctive dislike, and even distrust of everything Roman, simply because it is such. The victims of this spiritual disease, for we can call them by no other name, would be the men to hold on to the old diocesan liturgies, and to oppose the introduction of the Roman breviaries and missals, while, at the same time, they not only are Catholic in heart and soul, but in principle may be indissolubly united to the centre of unity, and even *ultramontane* in conviction as to the doctrine of the infallibility of the Head of the Church.

It is easy enough to characterize a body, it is not at all so to determine when an individual belongs to it, especially when it is question not of a set system of doctrine, but of a certain class of sympathies. You can come at the doctrine a man professes much more easily than at the state of his feelings. The only safe means of knowing the latter is to note his usual line of conduct; and still better, if possible, to observe his general mode of speaking, touching the subject, or cause in question, or his private treatment of little details connected with it. Now, judging of M. Carriere's sympathies by this sure test, which a close intercourse of some years enables us to apply in his regard, we have not the least doubt but that even in this second and least objectionable sense of the word, the late Superior of St. Sulpice was by no means a Gallican. In his mouth, the Head of the Church was "the Holy Father," or, *le tres Saint Pere;* or still more tenderly, *Notre Saint Pere le Pape;* or in sign of profound respect, "the

Sovereign Pontiff;" and the Papal court was invariably referred to as that of the "Holy See;" while with your sympathetic Gallican, the former is always "the Pope," and no more; and the latter, "Rome," or the "Court of Rome." That is to say, the general tenor of M. Carriere's language towards the Holy See was not characterized by the respectful coldness of the Gallican (counterpart of the respectful silence of the Jansenists), but by the cordial veneration, warmth, and even tenderness of the thorough-going Catholic, or, as English phraseology has it, of the "ultramontane" priest.

Your modern Gallican (of course leaving the Head of the Church himself untouched) is invariably given, if of a humourous temperament, to indulging in little freaks of wit and fancy at the expense of the Papal court and the Pope's *entourage;* or, if he be of a serious turn, to making vexed complaints of decisions of the " Congregations," and sighing over their supposed slips and imprudent steps: he is fond of dwelling with an evident relish on stories not over complimentary to the "Court of Rome," and is often found touching upon half-told scandals of the same, always with a certain air of mystery, as if more could be said if it were prudent. Now, in M. Carriere we never observed the least tendency to anything of this kind, although hearing him daily (at spiritual lecture in the evening) speak on all manner of religious subjects; on the contrary, we used to notice that his remarks in connexion with the Holy See, while invariably serious, and calculated to inspire profound respect of that supreme Christian power, were very often marked by a peculiar tenderness which he manifested on few other subjects. The reason of this was, doubtless, the very distressing position of the Holy Father, and the gloomy prospect of Roman affairs at the time, for it was during the disasters of the late Italian war. As Holy Writ says of the priest Samuel: "In his *words* he was known to be faithful;" nor would his *acts* lead to a different conclusion.

We happened to be still in St. Sulpice at the time of the old Superior's return from his first visit to the Eternal City. Naturally all in the house were most anxious to learn the great theologian's impressions of "Rome and its rulers." He published them, the evening after his arrival, in the "great hall" of the college; when it appeared that he was charmed with the Pope, and delighted with the Holy City. One of his remarks, in particular, will long remain fixed in the memory of those who sat there that evening. Referring to the Holy Father, "We knew him," he said, "to be a great and good Pope, and we certainly did expect to find in him a holy man, but we have found in him a *saint!*" With truly French delicacy of feeling, he then presented every student with a medal bearing a likeness of Pope Pius, to preserve and to wear, not only as a *souvenir* of the occasion, "but," said he, "to foster a lively devotion to the person of our most Holy Father." This little trait reveals the real state of Carriere's feelings towards the Holy See far better than a more pretentious "demonstration," or than public declarations of sympathy could possibly do; these, however, are not wanting.

As we have seen, when only a student he gave early proof of his heartfelt allegiance to the Sovereign Pontiff; and the same feeling followed him through life. He had not often an occasion of giving public proof of it; but whenever an opportunity did present itself he was always found to show himself on the "right side." Take, for instance, his declared opposition to the organic articles tacked on to the concordat by the government of the First Consul without the consent of the Pope; and again, his active interference on behalf of the authority of Rome, in the debates which arose in connexion with the practical consequences of the concordat, particularly in the question of the extent of episcopal power in granting dispensations. On these different occasions M. Carriere took care to expose, and with all the weight which universal confidence in his great learning gave to his words, to denounce the danger into which he feared the French bishops were likely to fall, of attributing to themselves too much authority, to the detriment of the supreme authority of the pastor of pastors; "for," says a contemporary, "the Superior of St. Sulpice was most jealous of any encroachment on the privileges of the Holy See."

At the time of the invasion of the Papal States* he drew up an address, expressive of the deepest sympathy in the wrongs of the "Father of the faithful," and couched in terms of peculiar tenderness towards the person of Pius IX. himself. Having

* A homely proverb asserts that the wind which blows no good in any quarter must needs be a most objectionable wind indeed, and rather insinuates that such an all-evil blast is happily of very rare occurrence. Certainly, it was a great evil, that storm which, from the dark Alpine regions of North Italy, rushing unexpected down on the once happy Papal States, spread massacre and devastation around, and, rooting them up from their bed of ages, tore some of the states away from that throne to which, during centuries of comparative happiness and peace, they had been united. The same storm, however, with a sort of whirlwind motion, blew back in return such treasures of affection and chivalrous devotion, such a very shower of fond hearts and devoted souls to the foot of that Papal throne, especially from the neighbouring land of France, whence it was most desirable to see them come, that the misfortune lost not only much of the sorrow it was calculated to beget, but even much of its evil; so that, in fact, it may be said, for what the Holy See temporarily lost in temporal power, it has been in part repayed by the lasting increase and generally renewed vigour of its spiritual kingdom. Not but that, at the same time, the sub-Alpine wind in question, was, of its own nature, a most detestably withering blast.

had the document signed by all the professors and students of St. Sulpice, he had it presented to the Holy Father in the name of the society and community over which he presided.*

During his presidency, as well as through his active instrumentality, the Roman liturgy was introduced into all the seminaries of St. Sulpice throughout France; and he obtained that by special privilege the Roman Office should be recited by all the priests of his Society, notwithstanding the peculiarities of the dioceses in which they may happen to be placed. In Paris, for instance, whilst in the college of St. Sulpice, which is the diocesan seminary, Mass began to be said and the office recited according to the Roman rite, the old Parisian missal and breviary were retained, and we believe are still in use throughout the rest of the diocese.

Again, although the society of St. Sulpice was, from time to time, virtually acknowledged and frequently even favoured with singular privileges by the Holy See, its late superior could not rest satisfied until it was confirmed by the positive and express approval of the Head of the Church. For this purpose, as well as to lay the homage of his

* The author was one of those whose signature was affixed to the document in question: he can therefore on his own authority vouch for its existence, which he does the more gladly that, with true Sulpicean reserve, the address was never published, or even the fact of its having been drawn up made known through the press.

filial devotion at the feet of the Holy Father, he twice paid a visit to Rome. So anxious did he always show himself, by every possible means, to bind the society which had entrusted itself to his guidance still closer and closer to the centre of unity and the immovable rock of orthodoxy. All this looks very unlike the conduct of a Gallican, but very like that of a disciple of the great Roman theologian, Muzzarelli, or that of a successor of the great Roman champion, L'Abbe Emery. Well, then, may we say of M. Carriere, that not "in his words" alone, but in his *acts* and in his *life* he was "known to be faithful."

If Gallicans in doctrine are an extinct race, and those whose anti-Roman and ultra-national sympathies have branded them with the same name, are nearly so, there has formed itself instead a certain party within the existing body of the French clergy which somewhat resembles the sympathetic Gallican class. Gallican is now an odious epithet in France, perhaps, as much as elsewhere, and not even the most advanced clergyman of the party we refer to would feel himself complimented by being so styled; nor, indeed, could he in strict justice be so called, for his doctrine on the Pope's infallibility is, in all probability, the ultramontane one, and he professes unbounded affection for the person of the Holy Father, as well as sincere devotion to the best interests of the Holy See. Yet, if you watch him closely, you will observe much about the man that savours of the old Gallican. It is not easy to determine it exactly—with some it will be one thing, with others, another; but amongst the most general characteristics of the class may be noticed a certain restless fear of the Pope which is not reverence, a half-expressed distrust of Papal decisions, and an instinctive dislike to Papal interference, as a rule; all coloured by an ill-disguised jealousy of "Rome," and a corresponding party or family feeling towards France. This last is the prominent feature in his system, if system it can be called which is far less the result of principle than of feeling, the which feeling is that overweening nationalism to which we referred in the opening of this chapter, and in which we have thought fit to place the source of all the faults of the Church of France, past and present. This ultra-French party has, by opposition, given rise to another, which shows itself in some respects rather ultra too—but on the safe side, for it is ultra-Roman; or it might be more correct to say, that the manifestations of the first have provoked counter manifestations from the second, or *vice versa*, rather than that one party was the origin of the other's existence.

Naturally, the very French division pleases the government better than the very Roman, and is also better viewed by lay authorities in general, even those of the purely intellectual class, such as *Messieurs de l'Accademie*. Were we to strike out the characteristic features of both parties, we should say the first is more literary—that is, more academical, and rather secular in its tastes; the second, more theological and very ecclesiastical; the first, more liberal (as the word is now taken), more modern, and original in its ideas; the second, more conservative and more traditional in its views; the first, more national; the second, more unrestrictedly Catholic; the first (and one cannot help being struck by this fact) is decidedly somewhat worldly; the second, as decidedly religious; the *Correspondent* may be regarded as a faithful interpreter of the views and aspirations of the first; the *Monde*, as the principal organ of the second; and, finally, the first musters stronger and more respectably amongst Catholic lay celebrities; the second has for it the great majority of the clergy of the country.

While it is certain that ultra-French sympathies on the one hand, and Roman tendencies on the other, do constitute the prominent features and, in consequence, the characteristics of those two parties, it can be seen from the above sketch of each one's peculiar traits, that, besides nationalism on the one side and, as the saying is, ultramontanism, on the other, secondary agencies have been and are at work in bringing around the formation of both into the clearly-defined shapes which they now present. Amongst these is, first, that social agency which seems at work in every society and in every country—the tendency of men's minds to split up into liberals and conservatives, as we should say, into whigs and tories. Then there is an intellectual cause—the difference between the Academy, with its literature and its ways, on the one hand; and the clerical colleges, or *grand seminaires*, of the country, with their intellectual food, their training, and their notions, on the other. Again, there are political agencies—the opposition between legitimists, for instance, and imperialists, between republicans and monarchists, and so on; and there is also, to a certain extent, a psychological agent, which is the distinction between men's natural inclinations, according as they are secular or very religious, light and very tolerant, or austere and leaning to the absolute. A foreigner who has not been shuffled into either of the two parties, will fully sympathize with one side on some points, and feel inclined to be utterly at variance with the same on others. But it can be understood that in the country itself where the double party spirit runs high, a man's ideas on some questions (say the religious) should be much influenced and even changed by his sympathies in other ways, or his private convictions on other points, for instance, touching education or politics; so that a man may now find himself exclusively attached to one of the two sides, although in another period of French history, in another state of the public mind, or if he had been trained in another way from that which fell to his lot, that side would not be the party of his choice. In point of fact, at the present day in France most of the ecclesiastics of the country avowedly belong to either of the parties in question; and almost every priest takes the colouring of his views from one or the other.

All this proves that the religious question is less the cause, than the occasion of the two parties to which we refer. When an extensive society of intellectual men, a great mass of thinking minds, has been shaken by some disturbing agency, political or intellectual, civil or religious, especially if men's minds are shuffled together by some internal cause, it is an historical fact—we are tempted to say it is a psychological law—that groups, classes, and parties, must be formed, or rather will naturally form themselves. Now the late powerful uprising and immense spread of "ultramontanism" in the clerical body of France, coming in contact with its old national feelings, has proved the disturbing agency in its case, which shuffling up the pre-existing mass of political sympathies, social principles, and philosophical ideas, has brought out the two distinct parties which that body now presents. The presence of such a division at all, may seem a formidable fact to unreflecting observers. It is not, however, in the least so. Not only is this aspect of the French ecclesiastical sphere a mere natural phenomenon, all things considered, but to the Catholic student it should prove a most pleasing and a most consoling one, bearing in view the happy nature of the circumstance which occasioned it. Moreover, this distinction of sympathies and views is nothing more than a *distinction*, and does by no means cause a division in the clerical body. Curates working cordially together in the same church professors teaching and living together in the same college, religious of the same community dwelling in the same house, even intimate friends, living on terms of the most perfect cordiality, may be, and very often are, of the two different parties; simply because while their training was the same, their natural dispositions, or perhaps family sympathies, were different; or, again, because of naturally congenial feelings, the circumstances of their mental cultivation happened to have been unlike. Meanwhile, the clergy is becoming more and more "ultramontane;" Gallicanism is well-nigh extinct, and ecclesiastical nationalism is daily losing ground in the sanctuary. Local rituals, breviaries, and missals, have nearly all disappeared for the "Roman;" and the Church's eldest daughter, our eldest sister, *la belle France*, is to-day more thoroughly Catholic, more decidedly Roman, than ever she was before.*

While, then, regarding the fact in its true light, and giving it no more importance than it deserves, it is admitted that two clearly distinguishable parties, without in the least creating a division, make a marked distinction in the body of the clergy of France at the present day, the question must naturally suggest itself—to which of the two belonged the late Superior of St. Sulpice? The question is a delicate one; however, taking into account the immense influence on the ecclesiastical mind of France possessed by the body of which M. Carriere was the head, the question is too interesting to be passed over by his biographer. In reply to it, therefore, we believe we can safely say, the Supe-

---

* We have heard her lately, through the chief members of her hierarchy, make a solemn declaration of her views touching the rights of the Holy See, as we remember her to have done long ago in the days of Bossuet; but this time, the "*Declaration du Clergé de France*," is not made at the special desire, but in spite of the sovereign of the kingdom; not against but in support of Papal publications—publications which were not only not confirmed, nor even partly approved by the government, but absolutely and expressly forbidden. *Gloria in excelsis!* How times have changed!

rior of St. Sulpice belonged to neither of the parties in question. He never put himself forward, nor was he ever regarded as an avowed partizan of either one or the other, and the body of clergymen under his guidance has, without the exception of an individual, kept strikingly aloof from the rather warm discussions which, of late years, have occasionally taken place between the opposite sides. As to his private convictions, we say with little hesitation that neither party could claim him as its own. Of course, having no further authority for our decision, than our personal knowledge of the man, we are convinced that M. Carriere would not have thought of endorsing very many articles of the *Correspondent*, still less that he would have approved of all Montalembert's speech at the late Catholic congress; at the same time, we know that it would be wrong to give Louis Vuillet as a correct exponent of his views, or the *Univers* or the *Monde* as a proper organ of his sentiments. He was too much of a theologian, too thoroughly ecclesiastical in character, in tastes, and in the cultivation of his mind, to place himself in the rather secular ranks of the first; while he was too prudent, too calm of his nature, and from his great experience, too well acquainted with the natural aspirations of the human mind, and sensible to the exigencies of his time, to be a partizan of the other.

Now, right-minded man as he was, he must, however, have had his views well defined, especially on questions of such importance as those touching the extent of the prerogatives of the Head of the Church; and at the same time, as no man, except some wild original, is so isolated in his notions, that he cannot be classified, M. Carriere must have belonged to some class or other.

To what one then is he to be referred? He was of that class of men which existed before the *Correspondent* or the *Monde* had formed the parties of which they are the organs—he was a Sulpicean. What Monsieur Olier, and what L'Abbe Emery were, or would have been had they lived in his time, that was Joseph Carriere in his views of the proper relations between France and Rome, the Holy See and the world. Deeply penetrated with the traditional spirit of his society, he was thereby able to steer a well defined course, without attaching himself to either of the parties which in his time divided his fellow-countrymen. By his life of comparative seclusion from the world, and habitual meditation, above the national prejudices and ultra-modern tendencies of the one, he was equally exempt from the influence of party spirit, and the consequent exaggerations of the other. We may make ourselves more intelligible to some of our readers by remarking that if Bossuet and Fenelon did in his time represent the two shades of opinion, in reference to the proper extent of the rights of the Holy See upon the working of human intellect, or its proper action in the ecclesiastical affairs of France, M. Carriere would most certainly be found upon the side of the once mistaken, but essentially right-minded Bishop of Cambrai; aye, and would have sided with him for even more questions than the purely religious. This indeed would be only natural, seeing that Bossuet's gentle rival imbibed his views, and sympathies, on religious and philosophical questions in general, precisely whence the author of "Justice" and "Contracts" took his, from the teaching and traditions of of St. Sulpice.* Both strikingly outside the religious parties of their respective periods, Carriere and Fenelon present alike, with remarkable similarity, the characteristics of the Sulpicean school of religious policy—extreme dislike for disputes or contending factions, and a marked tendency towards conciliating opposition; but, withal, ardent devotion to God, above friends, above country, and above king; through God to his Church, and through that Church to its one visible Head on earth.

* Having studied in the same College.

CHAPTER VII.

ST. SULPICE.

Regularis disciplinæ zelator indefessus is one of the compliments which the gratitude of his society has engraved on M. Carriere's tomb. It is paid to him in his capacity of Superior of St. Sulpice, and for this reason we must see what it implies. To which purpose let us briefly review the features of that "regular discipline," to have preserved which in all its purity, during his presidency, is considered such a meed of praise to pay to the memory of the subject of our memoir.

One of the first things to strike a student on entering the college, over which M. Carriere lately presided, was not only the exactness, but the cheerfulness with which the college regulations were observed, even in their most minute details. The rule of St. Sulpice is, as is generally known, one of the strictest of our collegiate institutions, and is moreover, perhaps, the most complicated, as it provides for the smallest details of a student's life, and leaves very little to chance or caprice. It is a most intricate machinery of direction. Yet a very large community (numbering about 300 theologians in the senior house at Paris) works under it with the ease of a well ordered machine. Everything goes like clock-work, not only as to perfect order and regularity, but with almost the same kind of automaton action. There seems no impelling power; yet all goes the right way, apparently of its own accord. There is very little active supervision to ensure observance of rule; there are no deans, nor are there any specially appointed substitutes for them. Yet the strict code of college regulations is observed with a punctuality, and universal exactitude, which have the name of being without parallel in any other similar establishment of education.

Again, the usual incentives to study are not here made use of; they are not found necessary, and would be considered unsuited to the general plan on which the house is worked. The calls in class are not in themselves, nor in their results, of a nature to be much dreaded, and are not, therefore, calculated to prove strong motives to study merely for the sake of meeting them; while that most powerful stimulus to youthful energy, emulation, is not only not employed, but is rather purposely discouraged. No prizes are given for superior answering in the examinations held at the end of each academical term. The result of a student's success on these occasions is not even made public, and may only be known by himself on applying for the note awarded to him. The oral examinations are passed in presence of the entire college, but the result in each case can only be a matter of surmise: then the success of the written thesis which mainly decides the success of the whole, is known only to the examiners. Among the students, therefore, there are no such distinctions as prize men, first-class men, second-class men, and the like; there are no honours to be won, no reputation to be gained, or, once acquired, to be maintained; in a word, no human motives for labour are held out to the young levites who study there. Yet, in few colleges, lay or clerical, are lessons better prepared, while those who have been able to test for themselves the general merit of the oral examinations, and have had opportunities of comparing them with others witnessed elsewhere, to our certain knowledge invariably observe, that they never witnessed similar exhibitions so satisfactory on the whole. It is a common observation of persons assisting at the examinations of St. Sulpice for the first time, that while there is not much brilliant display, there appears almost universal excellence—an excellence which, while it seldom rises much above, in few cases falls below that degree known as satisfactory. How are these desirable results obtained? How, to take for instance the senior house at Paris, is its community of 300 young men, and hot-headed, light-hearted Frenchmen too, made to observe a strict rule without almost any supervision, without the active vigilance of a single dean? And how is the same body made to study so perseveringly, and so well, without the help of the ordinary means employed to stimulate and support the studious activity of youth?

The secret lies in what explains many things peculiar to St. Sulpice, amongst others, why, although founded as a house of education for the clergy of Paris, it has become a centre of attraction for ecclesiastical youth from every diocese of France, and from different parts of the world—why, although by right and pretension only a diocesan seminary, it has become a cosmopolitan college: and the secret is to be found in the exceptional *spirit* of the house.

For the very reason that it is at the bottom of almost every Sulpicean peculiarity, we have already had very frequently to refer to this spirit of St. Sulpice, and in doing so have brought out some of its principal characteristics, its devotion to the centre of Catholic unity, its dislike to disputes of any kind, and its marked distaste for publicity. It remains to name its essence, to say what it is in itself. This is nothing more nor less than what is known in spiritual phraseology as purity of intention. It is a lively impression that God is being served, and a corresponding, efficacious intention to work for

His sake only, to do well what is to be done, simply because the work is His, in whose service each student is taught to feel he has enlisted himself, on the day he entered college to prepare to serve in His sanctuary. This idea, with the train of thought it suggests, and the tone of feeling it naturally gives rise to, is in several ways kept alive and active; in its different bearings, it is dwelt on in the morning's meditation; its practical consequences in particular cases are brought out at the mid-day's "particular examen;" and motives for general action are, as far as possible, taken from it in the evening's " spiritual lecture." In direction, and at the sacred tribunal, it is still further instilled into the mind; and the ordinary college books of devotion base their prescriptions for the health of the spiritual life on its supposed pre-existence in the soul: in fine, from the considerations to which it gives rise, as from so many admitted premises, counsel and precept deduct their conclusions.

The two festivals peculiar to St. Sulpice, the "Interior Life of Jesus," and the "Interior Life of Mary," which by special privilege are there celebrated with particular services, and kept with much solemnity and devotion, are in reality but illustrations of the perfection of its "spirit," as celebrating its presence in those whom ecclesiastical students most revere, and would naturally take as favorite models of true perfection. It is perhaps still more efficaciously illustrated by the living examples of the superior's themselves, who, although secular priests, labour in the arduous work of instruction and collegiate direction without salary or recompense of any kind; are just as simply lodged, partake of the same plain fare, attend the same exercises of devotion, and, if not strictly bound to do so, observe the same rules as those of whom they have charge; while, in leading this monotonous life of labour and self-restraint, many of them are clearly sacrificing brilliant careers and positions of high emolument that lie open to them elsewhere; thus, in their own persons, forcibly preaching that purity of intention which they endeavour to make the mainspring of action for the community which they govern.

By all these means is generated and kept alive a peculiarly active state of devotional feeling, which, with its vivid sentiments of the Divine presence, and its unmistakeable train of supernatural views, principles, and motives, constitutes what is known as the spirit of St. Sulpice. This "spirit" is certainly a highly supernatural state; consequently, one which would seem more desirable than attainable, and, if possible in a community of religious, hardly so in a body of young men just entered college, at that age when, in other professions than the clerical, begins the proverbially wild period of university life. But, as Napoleon says, fact has an incontrovertible logic, and the fact is, that the high supernatural state in question *is attained*. While it exists in greater perfection in the head house at Paris, it is found with its practical results in the other Sulpicean colleges, and, in general, in the clerical colleges of France, of all of which St. Sulpice is the prototype.

It is objected to that particular feature of the Sulpicean spirit which excludes emulation, and premiums for superior merit, that it must ultimately prove very detrimental to the activity of studies. So, no doubt, it naturally would in a lay college, but so it as naturally ought not in a seminary of advanced ecclesiastical students. Their experience of 200 years' clerical training has taught the Sulpiceans that to rivalry and prize-seeking may be substituted, for future priests, other motives of action less attractive to human nature, but more worthy of the essentially spiritual profession to which they aspire, and in reality quite as efficient in securing general success in studies.

Human motives are naturally the most powerful to urge men on in that great race of life which we call the *world*, but in that chase after souls which is the life of the Church, purely spiritual views are far greater stimulants. The priest whose ends in working are tainted with mercenary or ambitious views will be found actually far less busy than one whose intentions are purer, even though the natural disposition of the latter be not at all so energetic. Within the Church an essentially supernatural order reigns, a supernatural spirit is, therefore, the most congenial to its atmosphere, and, consequently, most favourable to individual activity. For all members of the ecclesiastical body, levites as well as priests, zeal *ad majorem Dei gloriam* is the best of tonics: others may momentarily be more powerful, or, partially, more successful; but none other is so safe, ultimately so efficient, or so generally satisfactory. Attending only to its stimulating power, witness history's picture of the Society of Jesus, in past and present times, for some of the wonders which this purely spiritual motive may achieve. It will there be seen that not ambition's insatiable desire, not the fiery thirst which search for wealth creates, not even the boasted power of carnal love itself, not any, nor all of the passions together have called forth such individual energy as zeal for God's glory has evoked among the sons of St. Ignatius. Now, while a spirit of emulation is but a legitimate feature of ambition, and anxiety for prizes but a purified form of love of gain, the spirit of St. Sulpice differs in no essential from the great impelling power of the Jesuit body; why then should not this "spirit" be as successful, in a community of levites, as that power has proved in the Society of Jesus, and like it do more for promoting activity than either honours or rewards? It may somewhat damp the studious ardour of the few ardent spirits of a college; but even in their case it fully makes up in soundness, what it takes from the intensity of their intellectual life; while experience shows that for the ordinary run of students, for the general body of a college, even regarding only its intellectual results, it is really the most efficient. Then, as for its ultimate effect on the ecclesiastical mind of the country, it is certain that no clergy in the Church presents such literary activity as that of France.

But beyond and above the intellectual advantages of this supernatural spirit of which we write, are the spiritual blessings it secures for the souls which it goes to nourish. A youth, throughout the lengthened course of his collegiate training, accustomed to despise even the most honorable incentives to action, when only human, because they are but human and merely natural, and taught to admit as ends worthy of labour those alone of the supernatural order, will eventually turn out a spiritual and interior man, and as such will find himself well at ease in that essentially spiritual sphere of action, with its almost exclusively supernatural hopes and rewards, which constitutes the life of the Catholic priest. Students trained to discard motives of self-aggrandisement or self-seeking in any form, precisely because such motives are selfish, and habituated to the thought of self-devotion as the proper spring of action, will, almost without an effort, become afterwards on the mission self-sacrificing priests, devotedly attached to their profession because it is the profession of sacrifice, and as such suits the peculiar state of mind in which they have been trained—its aspirations and its longings for self-sacrifice, which training has made to them a second nature. This high spirituality, and this eagerness for self-devotion, every one knows are characteristics of the French ecclesiastics; in particular of those with whose characters we are best acquainted, the French foreign missioners: however, every one does not know that these striking qualities of the clerical body of France are but the manifestations of that active supernatural life which the spirit of St. Sulpice has breathed into its members.

Now, we cannot claim for M. Carriere the credit of having infused this "spirit" into the members and the houses of his community, or of having diffused it through the clerical body of his country. If such credit be due to any individual, the honour belongs to the saintly, but yet unsainted, M. Olier, the founder and first Superior of St. Sulpice. Joseph Carriere does, however, deserve, and his society and the clergy of his country gratefully award to him the merit of having embodied in himself that spirit in its perfection, of having during his presidency preserved it pure from human alloy, and, what still more redounds to his praise, of having made its exercise more fervent and more active than he found it in St. Sulpice before him.

Although the spirit of St. Sulpice is the mainspring of the Sulpicean system, and the primary cause of its success, certain secondary features of that system may be regarded as contributing to its favourable results. The first is, that it works only through the better feelings of human nature, its sense of honour, self-regard, and self-respect. When observance of any rule, or set of rules, is insisted on by superior or directors, no mention is ever made of punishment, no assurance given of certain detection, no threats of any kind resorted to. When natural motives, are at all employed, they are appeals to the nobler feelings of the human heart, especially to that one which works so powerfully in a Frenchman's breast—the sentiment of honour. Twice a-year the rector himself delivers a series of lectures known as the "explanation of the rule." Each rule is then successively taken up, its purpose explained, and its advantages exposed. The wisdom of the whole code of college regulations being thus clearly brought out, an intelligent appreciation of its merits, and a consequently profound respect for its ordinances, is wisely spread amongst the members of the community; for it is an axiom of government, as old as the days of Lycurgus, that to have laws well observed they should be first well respected. As we already observed, very little active supervision is employed; the students are to a great extent left to themselves; they are taught to feel that considerable confidence is placed in their trustworthiness, and thereby they are taught to be trustworthy. While no show is made of watching for defaulters to rule, a certain amount of vigilance must be kept up; but in carrying it out there is not the slightest approach to a system of espionage. Violations of rule, when detected, are met in a fair, honourable way; in fact, from the nature of the system, appear of themselves. The students of St. Sulpice are not treated as boys still at school, but as young men who will very soon be priests. They are taught to feel that they are respected, and thereby are taught to make themselves worthy of respect. So that a stranger in this college will soon observe that a student is rather ashamed than afraid to be found violating rule. Indeed, fear is a sentiment unknown there; it would be abhorrent to the system of the house to give rise to it, much less to employ it as a means of securing obedience; in its stead, that system makes use of self-respect, and finds it far more efficacious.

Another feature of the Sulpicean system, which has considerable part in the attainment of the happy results for which it is remarkable, is the almost perfect equality it maintains between professors and students. When a young man sees directors, and teachers, whom he has learned to regard with sentiments of profound respect, and many of whom he knows to be eminent men, subjecting themselves to the same rule and the same routine of duties to which he himself is subject (monotonous as some of these exercises must be to them), and, on the whole, although working harder, faring no better than himself, unless his be a callous heart and downright worthless soul, he is necessarily debarred from complaining of strictness of discipline, or even feeling dissatisfied with things, of their nature irksome enough; while at the same time he comes to regard those superiors with feelings of peculiar tenderness: so that, with a sort of respectful friendship, learning to love those whom, as a student, he feels bound to obey, in avoiding violation of rule, fear of punishment is for him changed into the more efficacious fear of giving offence, where to offend is in itself a pain to the offender.

In the relations maintained between the professors

and students of St. Sulpice, beside equality we must place fraternity. The most perfect familiarity and freedom of intercourse is kept up between both; they literally "like brothers live together." Professors do not form a separate body in themselves; they constitute part of the community, seemingly less at its head than amongst its members. In the refectory, as in the college-hall, they are not separated from the body of students, but are scattered amongst them; through the college, their rooms are placed amongst theirs, and they always spend their recreation in their company; so that in its general aspect St. Sulpice resembles a house inhabited by clergymen living in community, more than a college of scholars and masters; indeed, professors and students are so mixed up together on all occasions, that a foreigner has for some time considerable difficulty in distinguishing one from the other. No peculiarity of dress on either side enables him to observe the distinction, and he soon learns that a youthful appearance is not inconsistent with the rank of professor, while a countenance indicative of "youth's season long passed by" may well belong to a student.*

* In the clerical colleges of France it is not very rare to meet among the levites the venerable fathers of promising young gentlemen or of marriageable young ladies, the said levites having become so upon the demise of their once better-halves. Lawyers

The heads of the establishment thus living among the students, as much with them, and as thoroughly of them, as if they were students themselves, it can be understood how naturally they dispense with these complicated systems of supervision and detection found requisite elsewhere; how, in fact, as we remarked above, is completely obviated the necessity of any special detective force at all. Deans and monitors are there superseded by kind superiors, who, always present amongst their students as friends and companions, are acquainted with their peculiarities of character, and conduct, better than the first, and share their confidence more thoroughly than the second.

In recreation hours especially are felt the great advantages of this freedom of intercourse. Recreation is the time when conversation on all manner of topics flows full and free, when the mind unloosed and off its guard, views are freely put forward and impressions quickly received. It is, then, of great importance that enlightened and right-minded churchmen, such as must be the professors of a clerical college, should mix freely with students, whose impressions on most subjects are still in process of formation. Besides, as in St. Sulpice, newspapers

give up promising careers, doctors interrupt profitable practice, in answer to vocation; either because their call was late, or having been felt long before, their obedience to it was tardy.

are not permitted to the latter, lest their attention should be diverted from the serious studies which engage them, their natural curiosity about passing events is satisfied by their professor-companions, who serve them like so many excellent journals, provided with news on all the current events of interest, and who may also be regarded as approved "organs," furnished with "leaders" on all the momentous questions of the day. The continual presence of their teachers during hours of recreation might seem a necessary restraint upon young men. That, however, would depend on the relations observed between teachers and the young men themselves, and in St. Sulpice no such restraint exists. There, the arrival of a professor into a merry group means an arrival of the latest news, a fresh supply of interesting matter for conversation (the Frenchman's delight), and consequently, fresh food for merriment. Professors are teachers in the class-hall, they are companions in the play-ground. A Sulpicean professor (spiritual considerations apart) has the good sense, and the good taste, to conduct himself towards his students as towards gentlemen who are about entering into a state which places them on an equal footing with himself, before the Church and before society. He naturally gets the first place—*la place d'honneur*—in every group, but gets only his share of the conversation; nor would he desire to take more, for the simple reason that he is not amongst pupils teaching, but amongst companions taking his recreation; while these are evidently under the same impression, preserving in language and manner all due respect to their superior, but availing themselves heartily, as young men will, of the privilege of thinking for themselves, and giving free expression to their sentiments. This familiarity between professors and students, with the freedom it allows to the latter, may not be advisable in the case of all young men; but it needs no great power of discrimination to see that it is so when the young men are advanced ecclesiastical students. When coupled, as in a well-conducted clerical college it naturally is, to proper spiritual training, its result must be to graft upon becoming humility that manly self-reliance, without which success in any career is impossible, as without it activity can never be brought into action. The training of the French student in this respect has no small part in developing that spirit of enterprise, that readiness in devising and courageous self-sufficiency in carrying out new projects or *ouvres*, which distinguish the French priest on the mission. Nor would the observation be too far-fetched, that this feature of French ecclesiastical training has considerable influence on French ecclesiastical literature, in rendering it so prolific as it is known to be. When a young man has been taught to give free expression to his ideas on occurring questions in presence of his superiors, and with their encouragement, and has been accustomed to find his sentiments not only treated with respect, but often even adopted by those whom he looks up to as eminent authorities, he is naturally led in after-life, when occasion calls for it, to readily give that publicity to his views which the press affords.

From what we have remarked of the features of the French or Sulpicean system of collegiate training (which, together with the humanizing spirit itself of St. Sulpice, must be regarded as accounting for that system's peculiar success), it may be seen that these chiefly consist in making students feel that they are really respected, and personally loved by their superiors, whom, in turn, as they cannot but respect, they are taught by similarity of life, and familiarity of intercourse, to regard with feelings of real affection. This, it must be admitted, is a very *humane* mode of governing youthful energy; but precisely because it is so, it is the best adapted to human nature,* and will succeed where more forcible but

* This nineteenth century has many glories to boast of, yet of none may it be so justly proud as of its triumphs in abolishing systems of force in favour of those of kindness, for training and governing animal energy, and thus making fear give way to affection, as a means of insuring subjection. This plan of substituting willing obedience for forced submission is as old as Christianity, and its action in the world is contemporaneous with

less humane means would fail. The Sulpiceans are not the first to have discovered that the confidence and affection of beloved superiors are favours which the human heart, even of its animal nature (bad as that otherwise may be), is extremely slow to forego, and that, whilst fear will produce acts of submission in many individual cases, love of the ruling power and enlightened appreciation of its commands will alone secure complete and universal obedience.

As we have not ventured to claim for M. Carriere the honour of having infused into the community of St. Sulpice the exceptional spirit which animates its members, we cannot give him credit for having founded the system through which that spirit works for the attainment of its ends. At the same time, as we have claimed for him the honour of having preserved the old Sulpician spirit in all its original purity, we must award to him the singular

---

Christian civilization. If modern society took in all other respects the same course that it is taking in this, it would, indeed, prove progressive; it would be becoming more and more truly civilized, for it would be showing itself more and more Christian. Christianity is the only road by which the world can travel on the way to true civilization: those nations alone are civilized who have walked it, and all others of the world, to-day, are either uncivilized or are sadly backward. Society errs when, seeking to make progress, it turns into any other path save that which He has shown, who is the WAY.

merit of having maintained the Sulpicean system in excellent working order as long as he had the charge of carrying it out. The colleges of his society through France were never more flourishing than during his presidency. The head house at Paris, St. Sulpice proper, as we may call it, sample and model, at the same time, of all the Sulpicean colleges, rather gained than lost anything of its distinguished reputation. It could never have been better frequented, for during the rectorate of M. Carriere it was nearly always as full as it could be. We are not privileged to enter into details touching the history of the society of St. Sulpice itself, in order to show the happy influence of its late Superior-General upon that body. Suffice it to say, it was only after long experience of his character and capacity that the Sulpiceans elected him for their chief director; their choice of him could not, therefore, fail to have been well made, and, from personal knowledge of the fact, we can affirm that to the end of his career they considered that choice a highly providential one, and their society blessed in having made it; as for our own part, we must add, well they may. For blessed, indeed, is that religious body which, when it loses the head that long had ruled it, can with truth engrave upon his tomb—
" *Regularis disciplinæ zelator indefessus.*"

CHAPTER VIII.

THE "ECCLESIASTICAL SPIRIT" OF FRENCH ECCLESIASTICAL TRAINING.

THERE is one point in the French or Sulpicean system of clerical training which we cannot suffer to pass without particular notice, not only for its intrinsic importance in the formation of the clerical mind, but for the very special importance which is attached to it in all French colleges, particularly in those which M. Carriere directed; we refer to the care with which the ecclesiastical spirit—*l'esprit ecclesiastique*—is sought to be instilled into the minds of students. This *esprit ecclesiastique*, of which French priests are known to speak so much, which French bishops, and superiors of colleges, are so anxious to promote, and which, therefore, constitutes such a prominent feature in the character of a French clergyman, is simply a turn of mind profoundly, and exclusively ecclesiastical. It is understood to be effected by a system of training thoroughly clerical, and, as such, so affecting the ideas, the feelings, the knowledge, and even the tastes of the individual, that the *man* is, as far as possible, transformed into the *priest*—will think and feel, and will, therefore, also speak and write,

only as a priest would be expected to do; so that
not only in his official capacity, but in the details of
his private life, the priest shall be unmistakeable
stamped on all he says and does. Everywhere,
Catholic clerical education shows a marked tendency to promote this particular psychological conformation, and hence the common reproach of narrowness and exclusiveness which is addressed to the
system. Exclusiveness, however, in the training
of her levites is but a necessary consequence on the
exclusiveness which the Catholic Church maintains
in the constitution of her clergy; who approves of
the latter cannot but approve of the former, the more
warmly the more it is perfectly carried out. By
imposing on her priests the exceptional obligation
of lives of celibacy, and the still more special obligation of reciting daily, and several times a-day,
those set forms of ecclesiastical considerations and
prayers which constitute the priest's office; by obliging them to adopt a dress always unlike, and
when her action is free, as in Catholic countries,
completely different, from that of the rest of society;
by even stamping their persons with the tonsure's
distinguishing mark—that shaven crown which outside English-speaking countries the priest's head
always presents, the Church clearly shows herself
anxious not only to separate her priests as much as
possible from the rest of mankind, but to make

them keenly feel the fact of such a separation; that is, to foster what we call the ecclesiastical spirit in her clerical body. It is, therefore, only natural that clerical colleges should show a marked tendency to develope it in the minds of their students, and if St. Sulpice, and all French colleges after its example, manifest a very particular anxiety in this regard, it only follows that they all the more thoroughly carry out the views of the Church, as to the proper spirit which should animate her ministers.

While this ecclesiastical spirit must, as we say, exist in every body of the Catholic clergy, it is most observable in French and Roman priests, because in both their cases clerical collegiate training is more completely ecclesiastical than in any others.* The French, by nature most observant of people, and the Roman Church, by necessity most observant of authorities, have both become deeply impressed with the conviction that the surest means of securing spiritual perfection in a clergyman is to make him sensibly feel the fact that he is a priest, and with all its practical consequences to realize the truth of what that means; and that, at the same time the safest preventative against heresy or schism in a nation is the existence of an active ecclesiastical

* Even before that period at which ecclesiastical studies, properly so called, are commenced, most French and Roman priests have been already formed in the ecclesiastical mould: in France, in the *petits seminaires;* in Rome, in the preparatory colleges.

spirit in the clerical body of the country. History teaches two great truths, first that no priesthood ever abandoned celibacy, ever yielded up its more than virginal honour to the call of passion, until first it showed signs of having lost its sense of sacerdotal beauty, and with it that of clerical exclusiveness, and manifested a general desire to amalgamate with the laity; the second is that no clergy ever fell into heresy or schism which did not readily subject itself to secular authority, thereby showing that it had lost its *esprit de corps*, its sense of priestly dignity, and with it its proper priestly pride. Of both these truths to form one, no clergy ever fell till first the ecclesiastical spirit died within its members, leaving the body a lifeless corpse, with power to stand erect no more.

The strange perversion of the English clergy at the time of the Anglican schism is an historical phenomenon, which every historian of the period has laboured to explain. Excessive wealth, growing thirst for freedom, and gradual relaxation of discipline, are separately or together given as the causes. None of these evils are strictly such, however: the first was only an occasion, the others were but effects themselves. The real cause was general decay of the ecclesiastical spirit in the members of the clerical body of the land. Only that this spirit, the spirit of St. Thomas à Beckett, had completely died out in England, her clergy would have never yielded spiritual allegiance to a layman, no matter what his dignity or his power. Apart from holier considerations, its very priestly pride would have scorned the humiliation. But above all, its sense of apostolic dignity would have scorned the idea of marching, priests and prelates, all under the command of a lady superior, and within its own sacred domain of doffing the mitre to the bonnet. England's priests lost sight of their priesthood, and through that first blindness it has been given to the world to laugh at the strange spectacle of a nation's clergy kneeling to an old woman, proclaiming her its sacred head, and begging at her hands jurisdiction to carry on the work of its apostolate.

Now, if the clerical body of England fell because it lost the clerical spirit, its natural support, that of France stood firm in the faith, because that saving spirit never left its members. The French clergy, with all its ultra-nationalism, always remained truly ecclesiastical, and, therefore, though at one time it became more Gallican than the English clergy before its fall was Anglican, it never ceased to be Roman and Catholic. Nationalism to any extent in a church is a very dangerous symptom, as showing a tendency to schism, but the royal nationalism of the Church of France in the reign of Louis XIV.

was of such virulence that the reflecting student of that period may well wonder why, under its influence, that church did not lose its Catholic life, and drop off the living body of the Church Universal. Its ecclesiastical spirit it was which proved its salvation, by then, and for years afterwards, counteracting Gallicanism, at first annulling its schismatic tendencies, and ultimately purging the clerical body, almost completely (as is now happily the case), of its noxious presence. Since the word ultramontane has been spoken—in France as in every other country, in the days of Bossuet as in our own—the ultramontane party has invariably been also the very ecclesiastical. No wonder that French bishops and French superiors should make so much of their *esprit ecclesiastique;* still less wonder is it that ROME should prize the same so highly, and it would be strange, indeed, if every anointed son of the Catholic Church did not cherish it fondly.

Regarding its preserving power in a clergy, one is struck by the remarkable coincidence, or rather the remarkable disposition of Providence, that the revival of the ecclesiastical spirit in the members of the clerical body of France should have appeared a little before the dangerous and lasting outburst of anti-Roman feeling which, during the 17th and the 18th centuries, Gallicanism and Jansenism occasioned in that country. It is also worthy of notice that the revival of this saving spirit is closely allied to the foundation of St. Sulpice, as the preservation of the same is acknowledged to be in a great measure due to its influence and example.

As the 17th century advanced, considerable apprehension began to be entertained by reflecting churchmen, in France as elsewhere throughout the Church, touching the spiritual state of the rising generation of those who were to people the sanctuary. The university system was the one hitherto employed in the education of clergymen. Aspirants to the clerical calling, during their course of studies, remained nearly as much in the world as students for secular professions ; they underwent but very little special training, and lived under no special discipline. Previous to taking orders, it was customary to spend a few days in retreat ;* but that same was not universal, for it was not always made a necessary condition to ordination. Time was when this state of things presented but little inconvenience, for

* It is well known that with the zeal for God's house which consumed him, St. Vincent de Paul undertook to secure at least that much preparation for orders, and opened a retreat house in Paris, where subjects for ordination passed through a short course of spiritual exercises and underwent a special training for the ministry. The priests of St. Vincent have, at Monte Citorio in Rome, a house of this kind, where foreigners studying in the Holy City who do not live in a regular seminary, are obliged to spend a week before the reception of each of the three holy orders.

amongst other reasons universities had been thoroughly ecclesiastical in character, in spirit, and even in discipline. They were now fast ceasing to be so in any of these respects. The language of the Church was being abandoned as their channel for learning; the sacred sciences were already at a discount in their halls, and were already nearly confined within the pale of the sanctuary, being cultivated almost exclusively by clerical students; while clerical professors were gradually dropping out of their public chairs; so that in all their features they were becoming as thoroughly secular as they were hitherto ecclesiastical. We but note the fact, leaving its appreciation to others, or to another time. Now, while the university system had become inadequate to the wants, its discipline and its spirit were become daily more and more unsuited to the special nature of a priest's preparation for the ministry. Unless some substitute were found for both system and discipline, or some potent corrective employed to annul their baneful effects, there was evident reason to fear that the clerical body would grow up with time more and more secularized, with secular habits, secular aspirations, and secular tastes, and so deprived of its proper ecclesiastical spirit, would find its ruin. St. Francis de Sales and St. Vincent de Paul, as, indeed, all the great and holy ecclesiastics of the period, with the ready, keen sensitiveness of true churchmen, when harm to holy Church is at hand, became painfully sensible to the impending danger. A general impression arose that the institution of what we now call seminaries was the only remedy for the threatened evils—that is to say, that now the only means of preserving the clergy truly clerical was to remove the levites from all secular influence, and keeping them in houses specially organized for the purpose, during the five or six years of their collegiate career, to add to the necessary course of ecclesiastical studies that of perfectly ecclesiastic training, and make it as indispensable for ordination. This great work, like all important religious or even social reformations, needed a man specially raised by Providence and specially adapted for the purpose. Such a man was found in the person of the saintly L'Abbe Olier, Curé de St. Sulpice.* His characteristic was intense attachment

* M. Olier is the author of several highly esteemed works of piety for the exclusive use of the clergy. One idea, that of ecclesiastical dignity and consequent ecclesiastical perfection runs through them all. His work on holy orders—*Les Saints Ordres*—which is the hand-book of French priests preparing for ordination, is little more than a glowing picture of the glories of the Christian priesthood. His idea of the proper formation of the ecclesiastical mind, and which is so well carried out by those who carry on his mission, was—make the priest respect himself, and he will make himself respectable. This is not the place to decide on the part M. Olier had in originating the idea of seminaries, and spreading the impression as to their necessity; certain it is, that he carried both into prac-

to the priesthood, with a lively appreciation of its exclusive privileges and requirements—it was a profoundly ecclesiastical spirit, so that Providence had clearly chosen him for the mission of its revival.

Since French seminaries were instituted mainly for the purpose of preserving the ecclesiastical spirit in the clergy, to develope the same in the minds of students is naturally made the principal object of their attention in training their subjects. This ought to be particularly the case in St. Sulpice; and so it is. To unsecularize aspirants to the priesthood, and make them as ecclesiastical as possible, was the object of its founder, M. Olier, and continues to be the chief object of its labours. *Ecclesiastique* is one of the first articulate sounds which the foreign student in St. Sulpice succeeds in catching correctly; he finds that word perpetually falling upon his ears in chapel, prayer-hall, class-hall, and refectory—everywhere it turns up, and nowhere more than in recreation, for there it is as much on

tical execution by the foundation of the seminary of St. Sulpice, and the society of clergymen known as Sulpiceans, for the ecclesiastical training of aspirants to the priesthood, while to this double fact is attributed the institution of seminaries in France, and with their institution the present vigour of the ecclesiastical spirit in the clerical body of that country. Olier's work was of God, and it prospered; and now every diocese in France has either a Sulpicean seminary or a seminary modelled upon St. Sulpice for the special education of its future priests.

the lips of students as elsewhere on those of the directors or the superior. It soon appears that the magic word is meant to express a qualification which, with masters and sudents, is regarded as the *nec plus ultra* of clerical perfection, and, as such, the grand essential of clerical education. As purity of intention—the "spirit of the house"—appears the principal means whereby the Sulpicean system labours to succeed, the " ecclesiastical spirit" is the principal end it seems labouring to succeed in attaining; and as the former is inculcated and solemnly illustrated in two special feasts, "the Interior of Jesus," and "the Interior of Mary," so is the latter "spirit" brought out for solemn veneration in the great Sulpicean festival of the " Priesthood of our Lord"—*La Sacerdoce de Notre Seigneur.* This feast is kept as a solemn major, and with an octave (although peculiar to St. Sulpice), on the 16th of July, that is to say, at the end of the scholastic year. As it is meant, it thus serves to bring forcibly before the mind of the students the fact that the end of their collegiate course is principally to acquire the spirit of the priesthood of Christ, without which, they are taught to feel (according to a favourite sentiment of M. Carriere's) sanctity in a priest impossible, and learning either useless or dangerous. While such is the training of French students, is it to be wondered that French priests should prove so thoroughly ecclesiastical as they are—not in principle alone, but in character and tastes?

As to the subject of these pages himself—the successor, and faithful imitator of M. Olier—the perfect Sulpicean, and, as such, the chosen Superior of St. Sulpice, could not fail to be deeply imbued with that clerical spirit for whose revival his house and society were founded. We could not doubt that Joseph Carriere was thoroughly ecclesiastical, even if we had not the particular evidence that we have on the subject. In point of fact, he has shown himself more exclusively so than would be possible or commendable in a priest whose mission was to come in daily contact with the world, and whose business did not, like his, lie wholly within the sanctuary.

See, for instance, the character of his intellectual labours. His writings (taking into account the large edition of his works) are very extensive; yet we know that he wrote only for priests, on subjects which had no interest but for priests, and only in the language which priests alone are wont to read. Now, though one production of a man's pen may not, the body of his writings may well be regarded as picturing his peculiar cast of soul.

Again, while Carriere was remarkable, and much remarked, for his complete indifference to politics, the reason was universally understood to be, because in him the Frenchman was sunk in the churchman, the man all-absorbed in the priest. We call this indifference to politics in his case remarkable; for he lived in a time of extraordinary political interest for his country, and being always in the capital itself, was on the very spot where political excitement rose to its highest. He was in Paris, at St. Sulpice, while Buonaparte still reigned Emperor at the Tuilleries, and heard of the great campaigns of Russia, Germany, and the Netherlands, as news of the day. He saw the battle of Waterloo followed by its changes, Louis XVIII. reigning king of France, and the country once more a monarchy as in the days of St. Louis. Another change, and Napoleon reigned again an emperor on an imperial throne. A second time, the Bourbons were recalled, and under Charles X. France was ruled by a Bourbon king. Then, revolution shook the kingdom; the monarchy was destroyed, and a constitutional government, under Louis Philippe, substituted in its stead. Again, a general revolution, and the country found itself a republic, now of one form, now of another, till finally he saw it sink back into an empire under an Emperor Napoleon, just as it was when first he came to Paris and settled in St. Sulpice. Thus were revolutions raging round him, and thrones destroyed and dynasties changed, and forms of government the most opposite succeeding one another before his eyes; but he, undisturbed in the general disturbance, like Him whose minister he was, looked calmly on it all, and contented himself with doing the "will of his Father in heaven!" Anxious only about the ways of God, he still remained "indifferent to politics," which means that his heart lay all in the sanctuary.

If, as we have seen, M. Carriere kept strikingly above or beside the religious parties of his time, it is not astonishing that he should have been still further from attaching himself to any particular political party. It is rather hard to find a son of the "*grande nation*" who has not made up his mind as to the legitimacy or fitness of some one of the many forms of government to which his country was at some time subject. One will be a republican, another a legitimist, another a Philippist, another an imperialist, and so on; but nearly every one makes it his duty to be something or other. Now, although (anxious to know the government of his predilection) we very often made inquiries as to what M. Carriere was, we could never discover that he ever showed himself anything more definite than a Frenchman—unless, perhaps, a Sulpicean; nor does it appear that he was ever found giving public expression to a positive opinion on any of the new states of things which arose, or of old ones which disappeared in his day. "*Mon Dieu, voyez vous,*"

Pere Carriere would say when obliged to refer to some occasion of political excitement, and with that peculiar accent and manner which we here recall to those who knew him—"*Mon Dieu, voyez vous ç'est un temps bien troublé. Mais il faut toujours bien prier que Dieu protege la France.*" Thus, although he was no politician, it would be hard to say that he was no patriot. "*La France*" might call herself "*La Republique*," "*Le Royaume*," "*l'Empire;*" for him she was "*La Patrie*" always, and his line of policy towards her still the same—always to pray, "*Que Dieu protege la France.*"* L'Abbe Carriere was not the only model priest whose political action was simply to "hope and pray;" and politicians, we believe, agree that a country is seldom the worse for such being the only kind of political interference on

---

* On some occasion of great political commotion in Paris (probably the Revolution of February, 1848), when the revolutionary mobs, in their zeal for the subversion of authority, were rather unscrupulous about rough-handling its supposed representatives, and a clerical garb might prove as dangerous to the wearer as a full suit of royal regimentals, L'Abbe Carriere (amongst others) was forced to abandon cincture, soutane, and priest's rabat, to put himself under the protection of secular "shorts." His costume on the occasion was admirably calculated to deceive the spectator as to his real character, having been, it is said, in the hurry of the moment, supplied for the purpose by the college *baker*. Yet the disguise, it appears, proved a complete failure. The dress was clearly that of a baker, but the wearer as evidently one whose experience was confined to manipulating the spiritual

the part of its clergy; while it is certain that the clergyman who confines himself thereto is never regarded as for that, the less faithful in his duty towards fatherland. So true it is, that the more priestly a priest remains, the more is he what he should be in all, even to his social relations, and the more, accordingly, is society forced to approve of the part he plays.

leaven in some capacity or other. Indeed, not only was he evidently an ecclesiastic or religious person of some kind, but even did in bearing, look, and gait, show forth those peculiar traits which, to French discrimination, determine the perfectly cognizable character of the *saint homme*. Doubtless, he did his best to play the part he was forced to assume; but the fact is, though his life lay on it, Pere Carriere could not get over his *modestie ecclesiastique*, or look otherwise than ecclesiastical, so thoroughly was he so in reality.

CHAPTER IX.

CONCLUDING PARTICULARS OF M. CARRIERE'S LIFE.—
HIS DEATH.

PART of the epitaph on M. Carriere's tomb informs us that during his presidency the direction of the parish of St. Sulpice was restored to his society: *"quo Superior societas in regimine parœciœ Sti. Sulpitii redintegrata est."* Of the different parishes of Paris, that of St. Sulpice is the most edifying: there the Sabbath is most exactly observed, the sacraments are most frequented, and those *ouvres* which constitute such a feature in the spiritual life of every French parish—the good works of religious societies and confraternities are most flourishing.*

* What in particular seems to render the parish of St. Sulpice superior to every other parish of the capital, and, indeed, of the empire, is its famous organization for religious instruction, known as "*les Catechismes de St. Sulpice.*" This is a vast and most complicated organization; and has departments for all classes and ages: it is worked by a body of the students of the adjacent college of St. Sulpice; who, without interfering much with their studies (for the catechetical business is transacted on Sundays), acquire thereby a practical missionary experience in "teaching the Word," such as, but for it, few could ever hope to attain. A short time since, a paragraph in reference to these "*Catechismes*," went the round of the papers; it was headed "a Religion of Charity," and originally appeared in an English Protestant paper,

The reason is known to be because the parish is exclusively in the hands of the Sulpiceans. It ceased to be so for some time, but the result was so unsatisfactory that it was gladly restored to their direction. Besides, it was admitted to belong to them by a very peculiar right. Their founder, M. Olier, was parish priest of St. Sulpice; and when he instituted the congregation of priests, called after the parish, Sulpiceans, by special privilege, while remaining at their head as superior-general, he was permitted to retain his parish, and the right of governing the same was handed over to his society; so that it was un-

where it formed part of the letter of a Paris correspondent, and gave his experience of a certain department of the "Catechisms of St. Sulpice," for the benefit of the very poor among the working classes. The details there given are certainly very edifying, and no wonder that one accustomed to the indifference of Anglican clergymen for the poor, should be deeply impressed by them. However, those ecclesiastics whose "tenderness and delicate consideration for the feelings of their poor *protegès*," the writer extols so highly, are not clergymen, as he gives them, but clerical students from the neighbouring college. The results of this catechetical organization of St. Sulpice are so remarkable that it has been imitated all over France, in Canada, and to a great extent in the United States of America. A professor of the college has written a large work exposing the system, its advantages, and the means of working it with success; it is hardly possible, however, that it could be elsewhere brought to anything like the perfection to which it is carried in St. Sulpice; for very few churches indeed, if any, could afford a teaching staff so efficient as the great body of trained students which works it there.

derstood that for the future the parish priest and curates of St. Sulpice should be members of the Society of the Sulpiceans. The Revolution interrupted this order of things, as it did the proper order of everything in the country : little wonder that it should have deprived the Sulpiceans of their church and parish, since for a considerable period it completely deprived divine worship of the church itself, and desecrated it to worse than secular uses. During the Reign of Terror it was styled, and treated as, the Temple of Victory : it then became the principal temple of the mock religious sect called Theophilanthropes; and as late as the 15th November, 1799 (or to employ revolutionary counting, on the 15th Brumaire, in the year 8th), a banquet was, by subscription, given within its sacred precincts to General Buonaparte. All through, however, the piety of its parishioners, by many little devices, preserved it free from those injuries which revolutionary vandalism wrought in similar edifices elsewhere, and the observant visitor can now discover in no detail of its superb interior any trace of its ever having been used for other purposes than as a " Temple of the Living God," or been ill treated because it was so. For the rest, all now (say the old parishioners) goes on there as of old : its priests are Sulpiceans, and the neighbouring college of St. Sulpice weekly pours forth its hundreds of levites to add to the power of its choir, and the efficiency and grandeur of its solemn functions : which happy state of things, while it was restored during the presidency of M. Carriere, was most probably also brought about through his active instrumentality.

Since ever he left his chair in the *grand cours* of St. Sulpice, M. Carrriere was almost exclusively taken up with the direction of his society, and affairs appertaining to the administration of its many colleges. He had little time to consecrate to his favourite studies of theology and law. However, he could not be said to have wholly abandoned their cultivation. His own tastes would have forbidden him to do so, and the good sense of his country did not permit it. His learning as a theologian and canonist, and his skill as a casuist, particularly in all cases (very numerous in France) where divine and civil law come to an encounter, were too well known not to be often turned to account by "inquiring friends." Being, as he was, a generally received authority on most matters of ecclesiastical learning, and as famous for prudence of character as for intellectual power, he was the great ecclesiastical referee of the empire. Bishops for the direction of their dioceses, parish priests for the administration of their parishes, and curates for those interminable cases of conscience which young curates are so ingenious in devising, and so unfortunate as to be continually beset with, until their own consciences get practically seasoned, all turned to the author of "Justice," and "Contracts," for satisfactory decisions. Whatever may have been his private feelings, the good will he always manifested in replying to their queries, encouraged these consultations, as did the invariably satisfactory nature of his answers. Moreover, the majority of the clergy of the country regarded him as a personal acquaintance, either for having been under his direction in the head house of St. Sulpice at Paris, or having met him while students in some of the different colleges of the society, or having come to "know" him on some occasion or other.*

* A curious piece of French ecclesiastical statistics would be a list of the "great men" who (not to speak of former times), in this century, passed through St. Sulpice. Few names of note in the modern ecclesiastical history of France would be found wanting. Those two, for instance, which are the best known amongst us, Lacordaire and Dupanloup, would be found there, as would be two others of quite as great, though of a very different notoriety, poor De Lamennais, and Renan, the too famous author of the "Life of Jesus." A few observations upon the latter really remarkable man may not be here amiss. He was four years at St. Sulpice, without having been promoted to holy orders, nor did he ever afterwards receive any. Even for granting him simple tonsure, amost unusual delay was made in his case. Once speaking to an old Sulpicean professor of Renan's college days, we were informed that he was rather an exact observer of rule, and was a very hard-working student. "Why, then," we inquired, "was he treated with so little favour, and disliked, as it is said he was?"

Certain men enjoy the rather troublesome privilege of being taken as a personal friend by almost every one who succeeds in "knowing" them, and what makes their case still more unenviable is, that such men are invariably "known" to an alarming number of people. Father Mathew was one of these. L'Abbé Carriere was another: and there was not a diocese of France but had a body of clergymen, every one of whom set down in his own mind the Superior of St. Sulpice as his very particular friend. M. Carriere's very numerous friends, then, throughout the country took care that his learning should not be suffered to grow dull, and afforded him unceasing opportunities of turning it to good

"He was far from giving satisfaction," was the reply: "he observed the rule, but he seemed never to have caught the spirit of the house. There was nothing cordial, genial, or open about him; there was no understanding him : he used not laugh ; he did not seem in the least desirous of leaving, yet he clearly was not enjoying himself here; then there was a strange gloominess always about the man that peculiarity of character did not suffice to explain." This strange psychological state we afterwards heard explained. Renan was, like Julian the Apostate, of a naturally impious turn of mind. A taste for religious and controversial science, which was also common to him, with Julian the Apostate, joined to certain circumstances of early training, led him to become an inmate of an ecclesiastical seminary. Its reputation, as the first college in France, brought him to St. Sulpice, and, it is said, the rare learning of one of its professors kept him there so long. He had a real passion for the study of oriental and ancient languages, especially of those of them which are little known ; perhaps, because their account, that is, to the account of the said numerous friends themselves.

At the same time, more public occasions were not wanting of displaying the extent of his science and the power of his judgment. He was called to assist, with the title of "theologian," at the Council of Paris, and also at the Council of Rennes. "On both occasions," remarks the writer in the

inaccessible appearance and the air of dark mystery which hangs about them suited his peculiar cast of soul. Now, he found in the professor of languages in St. Sulpice one who could tell him more about these ancient tongues than perhaps any other man in France; at least, circumstanced as he then was, he could not have hoped for access elsewhere to a philologist of such vast erudition. So, we have learned, although a confirmed infidel long before his dismissal, Renan remained in St. Sulpice to possess himself of the treasures of philological science which intercourse with this French Mezzofanti afforded. Hence it was that he did not show himself "in the least anxious to leave," while he was clearly not "enjoying himself there." The spirit of St. Sulpice, with its tender piety, its lively faith, and its apostolic enthusiasm, must have been a sore companion for the already infidel soul of the subsequently blasphemous author of the "*Vie de Jesus.*" But here we gladly note a redeeming trait in the character of this unfortunate man: it appears that on the publication of every one of his works (for he is an author as prolific as he is successful) he sends a presentation copy to his former master in St. Sulpice. At the porter's we once happened to alight on one such left there by his orders. It was a work on the Book of Job, had just appeared, and bore in Renan's own handwriting a presentation compliment very flattering to his old teacher: that holy man would, no doubt, have well dispensed with both compliment and present.

Journal des Villes et Campagnes, whom we have already quoted, "after having surprised the distinguished commissioners charged with drawing up the decrees, by the power of his logic and the preciseness of his decisions, he still more edified them by a simplicity and a naive piety, which the most fervent religious might have envied." We had to make almost the same remark of his presence at the Council of Baltimore.

Monseigneur Sibour, Archbishop of Paris, founded in that city a sort of ecclesiastical debating society, or conference, to be held four times a-year, for the discussion and solution of all the most practical and delicate questions of the day, as many such questions, particularly of the politico-religious kind, were then continually arising. Of course, the author of "Justice" and "Contracts" was the doctor chosen as head of this society of theologians. To use the French term, he was appointed Moderator, that is to say charged with moderating the discussions, keeping them within proper limits, and seeing that, in the heat of argument, the point at issue was not departed from; as also after having heard the opinions given and the solutions proposed, and having resumed the arguments *pro* and *con*, like a judge after the hearing of a case, to propose his own sentiments to the assembly; which modest proposal, it appears, was generally equivalent to a settlement of the question, not only for Carriere's personal authority but for the intrinsic merit of his sentiment, and the logical evidence in which he was sure to place it.

Monseigneur Quelen, predecessor of Monseigneur Sibour, was very anxious to organize the Sorbonne, and render it what it is still far from being,* worthy of the theological faculty of the empire. For this intent, he thought he could do no better than lay his projects before M. Carriere, the more so, that in them that distinguished theologian bore a most prominent part. What M. Carriere's views on the subject were, we cannot say; but we know that he refused the highly honorable part which the archbishop had reserved for him in his plans of academical organization, and which he pressed on his acceptance in the most flattering terms. Probably he did not see in the Archbishop's projects sufficient room for the interference of the Holy See, or that he did not find sufficient security for the future approbation of that supreme teaching power: in any case, this was only one of many occasions on which the late General of the Sulpiceans showed himself proof to persuasion in refusing ecclesiastical honours outside the pale of his society. A certain minister of public worship, famous for his irresistible ad-

* Not being yet confirmed by the positive approbation of the Church's Universal Teacher.

dress, and specially delegated for the purpose of storming Carriere's well-known intention of not accepting the mitre, exhausted all his powers of persuasion with no other effect than to convince himself of the strength of principle and firmness of character of the man to whose resolution he was laying siege. "Why that man is more immoveable than a rock!" the minister of irresistible address is reported to have explained on rendering an account of the failure of his mission.

The invincible pertinacity with which the late Superior of St. Sulpice continually refused to accede to similar proposals, though occasionally supported by the influence of the highest authorities, civil and ecclesiastical, of the empire, and often made with considerable importunity, must not be attributed to a pusillanimous dread of increased responsibility, for acceptance would have diminished the amount of his reponsibility—nor even to a false modesty and overweening sense of personal unworthiness, for our knowledge of the man's shrewd common-sense sets aside such a version of his motives in refusing honours, of which he could not but know he was in a particular manner worthy. No; his motive for these refusals was characteristic of his general conduct, and was a well-reasoned conviction founded on sound principle.

Having become a member of the Society of St.

Sulpice, because he was persuaded that such was his vocation, having undertaken its direction as its chosen head for the same reason, he was convinced that he was called to be a Sulpicean at the head of the Sulpiceans, by that voice, to do whose bidding was the sole end of his existence; he was, therefore, resolved to remain so to the end: and hence powerful dignitaries and esteemed friends employed their influence to no purpose, and even irresistible ministers of state pleaded in vain to call him elsewhere. One man alone could have shaken his resolution, for the knowledge of that man's order could have changed his conviction; the order was, however, never given. He who might have spoken it, and been obeyed, aware of M. Carriere's character, respected his personal convictions, even though formed in *causa sua*, too much to offer them any violence: as also, no doubt, with the foresight which distinguishes him amongst distinguished Pontiffs, the Head of the Church must have seen that this powerful member was in its right place—that whilst the Superior of St. Sulpice would have graced any post of honour in the Church, he was best suited for that one which he actually held. Moreover, we may well believe that if some friends were anxious to see him raised to a more brilliant position, others, and likely enough those whose advice he most prized, showed themselves equally anxious that he should remain at the head of his society, because they could see none other so influential, or any one in which his learning and genius, or even his great talent for governing, could be turned to such account.

During the long term of his presidency (over fourteen years), M. Carriere never thought fit, from motives of fatigue or indisposition, to omit any of the duties consequent on his charge, not even one of his periodical visits to the different colleges of his society. Although in his old age (when he was closing on seventy) it would have been perfectly excusable in him to abstain from personally attending to some of his most laborious duties, for instance those which entailed the hardship of much travelling, he really never found it necessary to do so. By nature endowed with a sound, and even robust constitution, which excesses never impaired, but on the contrary, frugality and regular habits kept free from disorder, and preserved in its natural perfection, he enjoyed throughout the course of his long life the singular blessing of uninterrupted good health. Six hours before his death, he was so well as to be actually engaged in making preparations for a visit of inspection to one of his seminaries.

The attack which so suddenly carried this great and good man to his reward was an aneurism of the heart. His was, indeed, a priest's death—sudden, but not unprovided; in any contingency his final departure would not have been an unprovided one, for he was always prepared to leave; still Providence kindly gave him time to receive, in all their fulness, the last strengthening rites of the Church. After gratefully receiving which, and having fervently recommended himself to the mercy of that Master whom he had served so devotedly, and so long, having had even time to implore the intercession of the Queen of the Apostles, to whom, in the spirit of a true Sulpiceau, he had always shown himself tenderly attached, and having invoked the protection of his blessed patron, St. Joseph, he quietly expired, in the 69th year of his age, in the city of Lyons, on the 23rd of April, 1864, leaving behind him a name which must command the highest respect wherever Catholic theology is known, and which, as such, shall be spoken of and cherished when many of those with whose sound the world is familiar to-day, shall have long been forgotten.

CHAPTER X.

PERSON AND CHARACTER OF M. CARRIERE.

IN person, Joseph Carriere was somewhat above the middle height, strong-built, and well-made; rather full and heavy towards the end of his life, in earlier days his must have been a right manly form. His head struck the observer as remarkably large, his forehead appearing ample, not very high, but broad and full; his features, regular in detail, bold in outline, and steady in expression, while evidencing considerable decision of character, pictured a mind gifted with great powers of judgment, but with more of that faculty than of imagination, and so gave you, at first sight, the idea of one much more suited to be a philosopher or a theologian than an orator or popular writer. Marked expression of face is the effect of active interior working, be it of passion or imagination; hence, while Carriere's features were wont neither to kindle nor to sparkle, they presented no expression other than one of perfect calm. Neither passion nor playful fancy, but pure thought was the wonted exercise of his mind, and that activity of the inner man betrays itself outside by no change or working of the features, such as would in the end give rise to some striking expression in their lineaments. Nevertheless, without being able to specify by what precise trait it betrayed itself, a *"je ne sais quoi"* about his look impressed you with the feeling that you were in presence of a kind-hearted, indulgent man, of a soul by nature more inclined to the practice of mercy than of justice, much as the idea of that virtue is connected with his name—a superior after a student's own heart. This peculiarly pleasing, soft cast of countenance was much enhanced by a freshness, and delicacy of complexion almost infantine, which, thanks to angelic purity of life, temperance, and regular habits (we might perhaps add absence of exposure), remained with him far into old age.

Not exactly of a gay temperament, M. Carriere was of a quiet cheerful humour; never, we should think, attaining to a state of hilarity, he was, we believe, as little liable (even by natural disposition) to be much depressed by anything; on the whole, however, more inclining to the cheerful turn than to that known as mere equanimity of temper.

As a natural consequence of this trait of character, his conversation was never brilliant, but also never tiresome, indeed he was too sparing of it ever to let it be so; in which respect, we must confess, it was hardly in keeping with his nationality, as we would also say of its total freedom from pleasant badinage, that tinsel dress which suits the

French mind and the French tongue so well. However, as his conversation was invariably sensible and often highly instructive, it was always interesting, sometimes even amusing, for he would occasionally indulge in a quiet, dry, humourous strain, of which the peculiarities, all his own, used to afford great scope for the mimical talents and other comic powers of the "funny men" of the college.

In the professor's chair, besides the other excellent qualities which distinguished him, his *speaking* was all that in a great professor could be desired; but in the pulpit we should imagine he would have cut a sorry figure at best, for he was decidedly no orator; in voice and in bearing, in delivery and manner of expression, he was unsuited for such public speaking; besides that he was not what could be called eloquent. His soul was too cool, too calm, in the settled repose of its convictions, for that warm outpouring of feeling and that tendency to agitate, which essentially go to constitute the orator; while his mind was too exact in its views, and too rigidly truthful in its conclusions, to lend itself to, or if it tried, to succeed in, that high colouring, that artificial dressing-up of its subjects which eloquence requires. For these same reasons he was not a *littérateur*, and could never have become a popular writer. Feeling, passion, imagination, must be found warm and strong in the man whose writings would please or could move the people, while the one all-absorbing faculty of Carriere's mind was only judgment. This judgment, however, powerful and sure, deep and broad, at the same time neat and exact in details, joined to a memory though not quick, very retentive, naturally made him what he was—a great thinker and a great *savant;* his thoughts being directed to the study of conscience and morality, he as naturally became a great moralist; while his studies being made by the light of faith, the great moralist was a great " casuist," or to speak more correctly, a great moral theologian. That indeed, a theologian *par excellence,* Carriere was; and that, we are convinced, both by powers of mind and natural tastes he was of all things best suited to be.

Although his sermons could not have proved effective, had he tried preaching, which he seldom or never did, his *lectures* when given, as we remember them, to a select audience of say 300 theologians, were highly impressive. He aimed not directly at the heart, but he smote it through the head; he strove not directly to touch the feelings, but through the thoughts which his words awakened, and through reflections they conjured up, he often moved those feelings deeply. Those who have had the happiness of hearing his powerfully reasoned evening lectures, after spiritual reading or after night prayers, retain an undying impression of the force of the truths they inculcated, without the aid of rhetoric, and with only logic to enforce them.*

* One of these discourses now comes vividly before our mind, for it vividly pictures the MAN, the principles of his soul, and the spring of action of his daily life, as also it is a fair expression of the "spirit of St. Sulpice." It was given as matter for the morning's meditation, and was delivered, according to the custom of the college, after night prayers, in the semi-darkness of the prayer-hall. The subject was, purity of intention as the one great fructifier of a priest's mission, and the folly of any other motive for action through life than that one which the Apostle preaches— the furtherance of God's glory in all things. The text was: " *Tota nocte laborantes nil cepimus*," Peter's touching complaint to his Master upon the fruitlessness of his weary night's work, that, "labouring all the night through, he had taken nothing." Wealth, honors, fame, were treated as to their fitness for incentives to labour; then, those motives which the world, and natural morality would suggest as the most commendable, in college, desire to please others, love of science, and the pleasure its culture affords—in life's after labours, general philanthropy, abstract sense of duty, mere natural desire to do good, &c.; all in their turn were examined as sound springs of action by the light of faith, of reason, and common sense, but were all found to be useless for the reaping of lasting fruit; and the work of life's long night over, the disappointed votaries of each of these evil, or worldly, or natural motives, were made to exclaim like Peter, as for a sad refrain : " Labouring all the night through, we have taken nothing!" "And you, Messieurs," concluded the holy man, "take care that for the time that is before you, here, and on the mission you do not work like these, after the advice of the world or by the bidding of nature, lest like them, in the end, you, too, have to say: ' Labouring all the night through, we have taken nothing.' ' Seek ye first the kingdom of heaven,' ' Do all for the glory of God.' Thus, ' in the word' of the Lord, like Peter, you will be casting forth your nets, and when the work of life's

More eloquent discourses would, no doubt, have told better; but would they have suited Carriere's purpose so well? True, they would have roused his listeners into livelier feelings and warmer emotions, and would have even wrought more vivid impressions on their minds. But these feelings and emotions would gradually fade away with the fading recollection of each eloquent phrase that clothed them; and impressions, however lively at first, would die away with time, or with the change of scene into the stormy world, from that quiet college home, and the religious atmosphere which kept them there alive. While the profound convictions which the piercing truths of those calm evening lectures, with their cutting logic, furrowed deep into the soul, nor lapse of time nor change of scene may ever efface.

A peculiarity of M. Carriere which was certainly characteristic of the theologian and the professor, and used to afford considerable amusement to his acquaintances, as being the occasion of many quaint anecdotes, more or less authentic, was his strict argumentative turn of mind. It was believed that he always thought in syllogisms, and "made up his mind" on any subject quite in *modo theseos*—that

night is over, and the dawn of the eternal day shall have revealed the fruits of your labour, your nets (like Peter's) shall be found full to bursting!" Simply spoken, this discourse was neither a sermon nor a lecture, but it was indeed a subject for meditation.

is to say, that after having first exposed the state of the question to himself, he laid down in order the positive proofs of what he considered to be the most advisable proceeding, and only arrived at a final decision after that all possible objections to his views had been duly drawn up and refuted. His language was certainly highly scholastic in substance and in form, as, indeed, was his general mode of treating all subjects and cases that came under his judgment. For instance, woe to the student who went to seek a dispensation, or permission, without having his object clearly defined, his reasons ready, and solutions at hand for all possible objections. A Gascon once told us in confidence that M. Carriere's daily hour's meditation was nothing more or less than a regular thesis, of which the conclusions, logically drawn from premises first laid down, would be moulded into practical shapes, so as to form at the end the "resolutions" required to terminate such exercises.*

* Of the many anecdotes related as illustrative of this essentially scholastic peculiarity, one occurs to us which used to be a standing joke in the college. Our theologian, it must be said, had a natural antipathy to early rising, or, perhaps, it would be more correct to say (as in the case with persons so afflicted) to rising at all in the morning. However, even in unnatural exercises, practice makes perfect, and the unvarying practice of many past years joined to present strong resolution, had succeeded in rendering the required matinal effort enforced by the rule void of any, even of

This scholastic and syllogistic turn, an eminently useful peculiarity, by the way, for a casuist, and

the slightest difficulty. So that the five o'clock morning call to "get up" was invariably responded to by the old Superior of St. Sulpice with as much alacrity and natural ease as his own signal to rise from table was answered by the community, when the midday or evening meal was over. Indeed, it was known that he never failed to wake a minute or two before the first bell, and would have routed up the community if, by some combination or other, the great clock had stopped or the "bell-ringer" had chanced to sleep it out. One morning, however, he did *not* awake of his own accord, but was startled into consciousness by the sound of the bell thundering its unwelcome summons through the house. "*Est il possible?*" exclaimed the old man rubbing his unusually sleep-laden eyelids, and astonished at the fact that he was far from refreshed as usual by his night's rest; on the contrary, that he felt strangely heavy, and painfully like one still very sleepy. Was it sleep, however, or was it sudden illness? and, *en attendant*, what was to be done? The difficulty immediately presented itself to his mind as a set case of conscience; that, once present, he could not think of proceeding to its solution, otherwise than in due scholastic form, and, after a moment's reflection, thus briefly argued the supine theologian: "This is most extraordinary. Now, either I have entered on some serious illness, begun during the night, and of which these are the symptoms, or the bell-ringer has mistaken the hour, and it is too soon to rise. In either case I ought to remain as I am—and so I will." Having arrived at which sensible conclusion, his conscience duly formed and his mind at rest—that silencer of doubts and mental difficulties—sound "balmy sleep" soon obviated the possibility of any further objections, if, after such an argument, any were possible. In a few hours "tired nature's sweet restorer" had done its work, and the old man awoke, fresh and brisk as ever, happy to find his health unimpaired, and still more pleased, to one which in our theologian was the result of his casuistical exercise, the effect of his intellectual drilling, was brought into great requisition, and consequently turned to great account in the proceedings of the Paris ecclesiastical debating society for the discussion of cases of conscience, of which, it will be remembered, Carriere was Moderator. Rhetoric is considered, the motive power in debates, and so it is when the meeting is large and mixed; for then passion and feeling coming largely into play, eloquence is the proper instrument to work with, as warm sympathy, not cold conviction, will carry the point. When, however, the debating body is select, its few members collected and cool, reason comes most into action, sound logic is the principal agency in the result of the discussion, and truth will carry the day: brains and mind will be all-powerful against tongue and lungs, the little argument will set at nought the mighty oration, and the accomplished orator will prove powerless against the trained logician, especially if the latter be cast in that most sound of logical moulds, the set scho-

discover, on immediate investigation, that his nocturnal reasoning was sound, for that the bell-ringer, owing to some irregularity of watch and clock, having doubtless the same cause, had mistaken the hour, and had actually rung three hours before the appointed time. "I tell the tale as it was told to me." It may not be exactly correct, but it is very characteristic, which is quite as much to the purpose.

lastic method. In the ecclesiastical debating society, the old theologian of St. Sulpice must have been quite in his element, and as he there came in contact with some of the greatest minds of the French Church, the scenes must have occasionally been very interesting. Indeed many are the feats of intellectual prowess which his dry syllogistic method and general scholastic skill are related to have achieved for him in that enlightened assembly. Subtle antitheses would be formed by the philosophical spirits of the meeting, comparisons drawn up and statistics presented by the practical ones, striking facts brought to bear by the historical, powerful statements and impressive appeals made by the orators, and the question, covered over with a mass of highly important secondary questions, in guise of illustrating matter, would be left all undecided, with, probably, a general impression that a great deal was to be said *pro* and *con*; when, the Moderator's turn coming to "say his say," at his practised touch the obscuring illustrative matter would all drop off, and the point at issue be laid bare, while with his hard logic and his dry, cold syllogism, the old theologian would "strike a light"—such a clear light on the disputed point, that there could be no further doubt as to its real nature, and, consequently as to its proper solution. There are several anecdotes extant of long and complicated discussions thus settled, even when the most powerful ecclesiastical minds of the day had tried to bring the points to an issue, and failed, or (as is so often the result of a powerful mind taking up a subject) had succeeded only in investing the question with a more imposing appearance of importance, and in rendering its solution still more desirable, while leaving it still to be desired.

Once the debate fell on that most delicate of questions, the attitude to be assumed by the clergy in the politics of the period, particularly in regard to a certain impending crisis, or to certain eventualities which might ultimately occur. The point was highly important and highly practical, hence calculated to inspire the liveliest interest as to its solution, besides that its consideration could not fail to awaken active sympathies, and evoke powerful feelings. The discussion was therefore warm and, most probably, lengthy, and *de more* the doctors differed. On one side no less a disputant was found than the great Lacordaire, then in the zenith of his glory, for he was then in the full force of his genius. The policy he advocated was one for many reasons most dear to his heart, so he pleaded for it with all the power, the pathos, and the fire of his eloquent soul; the voice which " carried persuasion in its very sound," which was even then persuading into unpopular convictions the most enlightened assembly in the word, the *elite* and the intellect of Parisian society, now spoke to persuade a line of action that was already the popular one, while, moreover, owing to the nature of its subject, it was enabled to add to its own persuasive accents these words of magic power on a Frenchman's soul, and which Lacordaire could use so well, "*l'honneur!*" "*le devoir!*" "*et la patrie!*"—for the course he advised was the patriotic one. Now, a Frenchman will always be a Frenchman, no matter whatever else he may be, and, except a soldier, no son of *la grande nation* is so devoted to *la patrie* as a French abbé; moreover, we all know that the human heart does not change its nature for finding itself in the breast of a priest—at least, that it is nothing the less sensitive for beating within the sable covering of a soutane. There is, then, little reason to doubt that the soul-stirring appeal of the orator *de la patrie* found for the time a responsive echo in the hearts of his assembled brethren, which was going a great way towards securing the assent of their judgments, and so carrying his point. It came to the turn of the Moderator to speak. In a few words he explained the state of the question, exposed the point to which the controversy had now brought it, and then stated his own opinions. Carriere was at issue with Lacordaire! The result was not long doubtful. A sentence or two laid bare the stuccoed walls, and exposed the unsafe foundations of the great Dominican's imposing edifice of words, when the battering logic of a simple syllogism struck, and brought it in ruins to the ground. The project of the orator of Notre Dame was rejected by the assembly, and the opinion of the theologian of St. Sulpice was triumphantly carried. An old scholastic would have exclaimed: "*Vive le syllogisme!*" and such, say we, is the power of truth over talk, of the logician's skill over the orator's art.

Another distinguishing trait observable in our theologian, was the very serious turn of his mind and intellectual tastes. Of course this was natural to him; it was the natural consequence of the peculiar formation of a mind such as his, of which the most active faculty was judgment. At the same time it was a good deal developed by the habitual exercise of his mental faculties, always reasoning and proof seeking. He read to form convictions, and in what he read looked rather for what the author was proving, and how he proved it, than to what he was saying, and how he said it. Books, therefore, in which the author did not want to prove anything in particular, but was simply trying to say all he could in the most pleasing manner possible, and after the most approved fashion, books of mere literature, were not the volumes he would have cared to spend his time over, or that even taste would suggest as pastimes. With the duties of his presidency passing time was an occupation in which he could never afford to busy himself, even if he cared to do so, which he did not. However, he not unfrequently indulged in mental relaxation, but it mostly took the shape of a visit to the superb library of the college, where his peculiar notion of an intellectual treat would induce him to select from the ancients a tome of some of the glorious old fathers, or a treatise of the great mediæval scholastics, and from the works of modern authors some favourite commentator on the Scriptures, or the learned glossary of some great French lawyer on certain articles of the *code civile*.

The thinking reader will perhaps think with the writer that this very serious turn of mind, that this proof-seeking peculiarity of the great French theologian, is common to most of our great divines, and is nothing more nor less than an unquenchable thirst for truth.

If Père Carriere did at any time take a literary turn, either for the greater refreshment of his mind, or which would be more like him, to add a few attractive features to a coming lecture for his young men, he would hardly have thought of going beyond the fathers. The golden phrases of a Chrysostom, the flowery pages of an Ephrem, the image-teeming sentences of a Gregory, or the ringing periods of an Augustine, and such like, came fully up to his notion of belles-lettres. Which is simply saying that his tastes were as highly ecclesiastical as they were deeply serious. Such a decided ecclesiastical taste in the choice of his intellectual food, as in everything else, was evidently but a feature of that ecclesiastical *spirit* which, as we have seen, he possessed in a very high degree himself, and was so anxious to develope in his students, on the principle that without it learning and talents in a priest are worthless or worse. And, indeed, if the sanctuary does occasionally present the sad spectacle of men whom Providence made men of talents, or who made themselves men of learning, but who remain churchmen of little or no account, and comparatively inefficient priests, the reason is almost always because in such men is wanting that decided priestly turn which we have noted for forming so conspicuous a feature in M. Carriere's character.

As there is a something in the look, the voice, the manner, and even the gait, particular to every person; as there is a predominant passion in every soul, there is *one* distinguishing feature in every one's character. So it is, indeed, with all that is, and with every order of things that are—unconfused distinction in unbroken unity; for such is the law of nature, therein, after its own limited way, imaging its triune God, necessary prototype as he is first author of all that can be. More perfectly carried out as beings rise in the scale of perfection, this universal order, observable among all terrestrial beings, shows most perfect in man. Besides that mysterious fount of unity, placed in every human being, and constituting *personality*, there is a something inherent in each one destined to stamp its still incommunicable *individuality*. Shown forth in many ways, all constituting peculiarities, its principal expression is the *one* peculiar trait of character. What, then, it will be naturally asked of us before concluding this biographical notice, was Carriere's one distinguishing characteristic? We have already had occasion to notice it *en passant*, and, no doubt, it may be gleaned from much of what we have already portrayed of his character or related of his life—it was *simplicity of soul*, manifested in simplicity of habits, manner, bearing, and mode of speaking. Natural to him from the beginning, a sound ecclesiastical training and well-directed spiritual self-culture developed it with the progress of advancing years, while subsequent intellectual greatness, and the succeeding triumphs of professional success, as leaving it all unimpaired, served by the contrast to throw it into more and more pleasing relief. In early life this is what lent the sweetest charm to his character, and what, as we remarked when referring to his presence at the Council of Baltimore, among the many admirable qualities of which he there gave proof, most impressed and pleased the American bishops. This, too, was what, later on, as we are told by a contemporary, most edified the illustrious dignitaries assembled at the Councils of Paris and of Rennes, at which he assisted as theologian. Finally, in his old age, when lately he visited the Eternal City, this same unfailing *simplicity* it was which, while winning for him universal admiration wherever he went, completely dissipated whatever unfavourable prejudices may have been entertained against his person by those who only knew him as the "great French theologian whose writings had once been censured." "We really did not *recognize* M. Carriere in the person before us," was the common remark of professors and prelates with whom he came in contact during his stay in the Holy City. "It would have been more correct," observes a French journal,* "to have said that they never really *knew* what manner of man he was."

"Why!" we once heard a Roman professor laughingly remark to a French student, "your famous Carriere is like a *bon curé de Campagne*." "I don't deny it," retorted the sharp-witted Frenchman; "but remember that is precisely what every one says of the Holy Father." The retort was unanswerable, for the fact was undeniable, and indeed the same

* The *Journal des Villes et Campagnes*.

observation was often forced upon the writer.* In many respects, even in certain personal particularities, which though of little importance were not the less striking, Joseph Carriere presented much to remind one of Pius IX. In nothing, however, was the similarity so patent as in that beautiful simplicity of soul which we believe to be *the* one characteristic of both, as according to the teaching of man's divine Master, it should be of every perfect Christian. Besides himself, the one living illustration Christ brought before his disciples of the lessons of supreme perfection which he taught, was a little child, bidding them be simple as he. Simplicity of heart is the criterion which his written word mostly gives for real worth. In that wonderful panegyric, for instance, which the Eternal spoke to the powers of evil upon his servant Job, the first, the chief encomium is that he was "*homo simplex*," a simple man.† The world, it must be confessed, much in-

---

* Over and over we have noticed that whatever may have been one's previous sentiment of the sublime grandeur inherent to the person of Pius IX. as viewed only by the eye of faith on his religious, and social eminence; or whatever may have been one's preconceived idea of Carriere's intellectual greatness, as known only through his works and from hearsay, personal acquaintance, even that of a brief interview with either of the two men, left exactly the same impression, that of all things in the world the man was like that well known type of all that is unaffectedly simple, good-natured, and genial—*a fine, old parish priest.*

† *Job*, i. 8.

clines to treat this virtue as more of a weakness than aught else. But Truth has written that the world's ways are not its ways, and even philosophically speaking, simplicity is an unmistakeable proof, as it is nothing more than the effect, and natural expression of many other acknowledged sterling virtues. For besides that it supposes true humility and freedom from that bane of perfection, human respect, it betokens a noble independence of soul, which cares not to dress itself in airs or captious appearances to please its fellows, and, better still, a thorough truthfulness of character that, according to the old proverb, "*aime mieux d'etre que de paraitre,*" seeks rather to be than appear to be, or rather cares not for appearances at all. To any character, or any soul, such a feature lends a charm which, while it invites confidence, irresistibly wins affection; but where it is allied to real intellectual greatness, there is found the *beau-ideal* which untutored Reason itself would suggest of a perfect MAN; one to whom even nature's unenlightened instinct would incline us to give our fullest meed of love and admiration. What reason suggests and nature's better instinct guides us to, reason's Eternal Type and nature's Author teaches. What else is pictured in that noble portrait which He drew of his vicegerents amongst men, as he wished them to be, "*Prudentes sicut serpentes et simplices sicut columbæ,*" but greatness of mind, in order to do battle with the "wolves"—cleverness to meet the world's wily ways, characterised, however, by true simplicity of soul, as the Apostle explains: "*Sapientes in bono, simplices in malo;*" or which is substantially the same, "*Simplex et rectus,*" as the Church, in the very words of her written deposit loves to depict her saints and departed great ones. Well may we be proud that this portrait which the Type of all perfection has drawn as his *beau-ideal* of more than Christian, of apostolic perfection, is so common as it is in the Church, in fact, in its main feature of simplicity, is peculiar to her celebrities, in striking contrast to those of the world, or of the worldly-minded sects outside her pale. Naturally, therefore, it is with no little satisfaction that we dwell upon the fact, that in the person of the Church's reigning Head, the illustrious Pius the Great, as in that of one of her greatest modern doctors, Joseph Carriere, we behold the characteristic traits of an apostle after Christ's own heart—true simplicity of soul and true greatness of mind. Nor let us be blamed for thus coupling names which we freely admit, in point of veneration should stand so widely apart. Both are inseparably linked in our recollections of the past, as now to memory's eye, the well known forms of their owner's appear, not in the dissimilar brightness of their respective glories, but in the same tender light of that simplicity of soul, which, to our mind at least, characterised them both alike : it is with our recollections of Joseph Carriere and Pius IX., as with those of their respective climes—memories of France and Italy's sunny skies, that come not picturing the blaze of their noon-tide splendour, but revealing the more tender, dearer beauty of their sunset's softened glow.

As we best loved what once we knew, so, will its image always remain present to the thoughts, even while the recollection of its more admirable qualities lies treasured in the mind. Thus, while from personal knowledge of the late Superior of St. Sulpice, we are fully sensible of his claim to all those honourable titles which the grateful admiration of his society awards him in that delineation of his character and career, which forms the inscription on his tomb, to only one of them his name is linked in our mind—that one which, though apparently the least flattering, a true Christian taste has made to head the list, " *Vir simplex ac rectus,*" because of all his excellent qualities, the one that expresses is what made him most amiable in our eyes. And while to others he is the famous French theologian, or the late distinguished head of the great teaching body of the French clergy, to us, as to many who like us knew him, he can never be more than

" LE BON PERE CARRIERE."

www.ingramcontent.com/pod-product-compliance
Lightning Source LLC
Chambersburg PA
CBHW020920230426
43666CB00008B/1507